HOW WE CAN WIN

HOW WE CAN WIN

Race, History and Changing the Money Game That's Rigged

KIMBERLY JONES

HOLT

Henry Holt and Company
Publishers since 1866
120 Broadway
New York, New York 10271
www.henryholt.com

Distributed in Canada by Raincoast Books Distribution Limited

Parts of this book were previously published in the following publications: "My Big Mouth" as part of "The Year That Changed Everything," *Essence*, May/June 2021; "Practice Allyship" as part of "40 Ways to Build a More Equitable America," *Time*, May 13, 2021; and "Kimberly L. Jones: 'I Am Grateful to Have Seen the World Cry Out on Our Behalf Within My Lifetime'" in "Up + Rising," *i-D*, September 31, 2020.

Library of Congress Cataloging-in-Publication Data is available
ISBN: 9781250805126

Our books may be purchased in bulk for promotional, educational, or business use. Please contact your local bookseller or the Macmillan Corporate and Premium Sales Department at (800) 221-7945, extension 5442, or by e-mail at MacmillanSpecialMarkets@macmillan.com.

First Edition 2021
Designed by Omar Chapa

Printed in the United States of America
2   4   6   8   10   9   7   5   3   1

To my dear friend Brandi Saulter, who held me at the end of the "How Can We Win?" video and has continued to hold me up every day since

CONTENTS

How Can We Win? 1

Hood Girls Can Be Heroes Too 17

Four Hundred Rounds of Monopoly 31

Reconstruction 46

The Game Is Fixed 57

How We Can Win 79

Reconstruction 2.0 83

Nine Priorities for a Balanced Life 129

Hope Looks Like the Future 156

In Memoriam 171

Further Reading 175

Acknowledgments 179

HOW CAN WE WIN?

In 2019, I put out a call to action to my community. I made a Facebook event for a neighborhood cleanup where I was living in Bankhead, a community on the west side of Atlanta. Oddly enough the area was named after actress Tallulah Bankhead's grandfather, John H. Bankhead, an Alabama Confederate war hero and US senator. But if the name rings familiar to you, it's probably because of the song "Bankhead Bounce" by Diamond and D-Roc, and you may even know the dance of the same name. I didn't grow up there like T.I. (*I was born up in Bankhead, y'all remember me*) but for many years I called it home. The Facebook invitation read:

> The family-friendly event will begin at 9:00 a.m. Meet at the corner of Joseph E. Boone and Westchester on Atlanta's Westside. Practice stewardship with your child. Picking up litter is a fun, simple, free activity that can have instant results for your child and your

community. In two hours, we can make two blocks cleaner, free of litter, and a nice place for the residents to come home to.

As I walk through my community, I see wrappers, Popsicle sticks, newspapers and every kind of disposable on the street, sidewalk and gathered at gates or fences throughout the community. Even on a beautiful art installation we have. If you live here, you might get familiar with seeing trash. If you are visiting, you ask the question . . . "why?" Well, your initial response to that question may not be a correct analysis or it may not tell the whole story. So, as a resident here in Bankhead, I'm choosing to clean up my neighborhood, and I hope you'll take two hours out of your time to help me. I will supply any cleaning needs, including gloves.

Environment is a place where humans as well as plants and animals live. Keeping it clean and neat is our responsibility. It is necessary to keep our environment clean because we get fresh air, reduce pollution, etc. An unclean environment leads to a bad condition of a society, arrival of diseases, and much more.

Four people showed up. *Four.* I had hoped that not just people who lived in the community but people who were from the community would care enough to participate in making sure our environment was livable. It was important to me because I understood the effect our environment has on us psychologically and physically. I wanted this to be the first step in taking back our community. I didn't want to wait for gentrification to finally be the reason for a beautification effort. I had done the work. I had reached out to the city and gotten a big dumpster, and I had partnered with an organization that gave us all the cleaning supplies we needed. Four people. We did the best we could, and we got some things clean. But in that two-hour time, we barely finished three blocks, and needless to say, I was disappointed.

Fast-forward six months, after George Floyd's death at the hands of the police. Protests had begun all over the country, and my friend Brandi, an Air Force veteran, and I decided that we should join the front lines of the protest because we noticed, in the news coverage, that there were a lot of young people, but we weren't seeing our age—Gen X—out in the street. We're both mothers, so we know what that energy is, and we felt like it would be easy for things to get derailed out there with all those young people, the anger and the media. We knew the way most of us are raised in the African American community, people are less likely to make destructive decisions in front of someone like an aunt, an uncle or someone their parents' age.

The first night we went out, we noticed strategically placed bricks that everybody was talking about. Images of piles of bricks at the sites of protests across the country had been posted on social media: from a suburb of Minneapolis to Tacoma, Washington, and San Francisco. Fact-checkers later claimed these were left by construction crews for building in the area and it was dismissed as a conspiracy theory. We saw a young man pick up a brick, and I just walked over to him and tapped him on his arm. He put the brick down. We were right in thinking that while most young people were out there for a good reason, with no aunties and uncles on the street, young anger was going to be the driving force to determine what happened. So Brandi and I decided to be the aunties at the front line who made it less likely a brick would get thrown or that there would be property damage. We made it our business to be at the protests as our way of protecting the kids from their wilder instincts.

I'm an activist. I've spent a lot of time protesting. I marched with John Lewis, right after the killing of Mike Brown. I marched with the Justice for Georgia mothers—particularly one mother I'm very close to, Monteria Robinson, after her son Jamarion Robinson was killed. So showing up for the issues that matter wasn't new for me.

After a few days of being on the front lines that June, a filmmaker named David Jones asked me to do some man-on-the-street interviews with him for his documentary. He had been at the protests, but in different places than I was. On this day, there was a protest planned for later, but we went out early to do our man-on-the-street interviews because people were outside, ahead of time, setting up signs. There was one young woman who was making a beautiful flower art installation in honor of George Floyd and what was happening in the civil unrest, so we interviewed her. We were in downtown Atlanta, and we started at a corner where the CNN Center is located. The College Football Hall of Fame is on the opposite corner, and there are a lot of high-end restaurants in the area.

I noticed a bunch of middle-aged Black people—aunties and uncles I had not seen in the street (except for Brandi and me)—cleaning up. When I asked them who gave them the cleaning materials, they told me they'd bought them out of pocket. They had supplies to remove the graffiti and were sweeping up glass and boarding up broken windows. When I asked if they lived in downtown, most said no. They had seen that downtown and Buckhead, another upscale neighborhood, had been damaged, and they had taken it upon themselves to clean up. Historically, when there's civil unrest, the destruction happens in the communities where people live. In response to George Floyd's death, people had taken their anger downtown where protests had been coordinated. There had been looting and rioting, and these Black aunties and uncles had decided it was their job to clean up. To clean up property they did not own.

When I asked them why, one person told me, "This is not the way we handle things." A woman added, "I don't want them to think we're all like this." *Them*, meaning white people. You can see why I would be upset, right? I plan a community cleanup in a Black neighborhood, and my people won't show up for that, but they will come downtown and spend their time, money and labor to clean up damage they didn't do, so they look better to people they don't know? This is what slavery looks like in the twenty-first century. They wanted to show massa they was the good Black folks. It's appropriate that we stand for our rights and stand against police brutality, but some Black people are so concerned by the white gaze—what we look like to white people as they regard us—that they would try to undo the effects of the real and righteous anger the rioters expressed. But standing there, listening to people my age, who look like me, speak their concern about the white gaze and the way we respond to our own oppression, it made me mad. They seemed more concerned about the white man's property than they were about their brother—dead on the street.

Two years before, I'd stood on that same corner, after walking miles holding up the autopsy photo of Jamarion Robinson, a college student with mental health issues. Jamarion had been killed by police when they fired seventy-six rounds into his body, while serving a warrant for a crime Jamarion did not commit.

I already had an emotional association with the place where I was standing. And I could not for the life of me understand how Black folks could be so concerned about the white gaze that they would spend their own money to clean up spaces where, historically, we haven't even been welcomed. Jamarion Robinson was dead, George Floyd was dead and these people were more concerned about buildings that are insured, that can be replaced and that they don't own. The police have gone rogue and are killing us, but qualified immunity protects the police from prosecution, and we keep dying. But they were worried about buildings?

How crazy is it that it took the whole world falling to a pandemic for a wide range of Americans to react and take action? It took us having to endure watching a man press his knee on another man's neck for nine minutes and twenty-nine seconds for the world to wake up to the atrocities that Black people have been living since our arrival in this country? If you are Black in America, none of this is new to you. And yet, some people were more concerned about property, as if we haven't been shown over and over again that the social contract is void when it comes to us. That was the most ridiculous bullshit I had ever heard in my life. It set me off, and I started talking. David turned on his camera, and if you've seen the video "How Can We Win?" you know that this is what poured out of me:

> So, I've been seeing a lot of things—talking and people making commentary. Interestingly enough, the ones I've noticed that have been making the commentary are wealthy Black people—making the commentary that you should not be rioting, you should not be looting, you should not be tearing up your own communities.

And then, there's been the argument of the other side that we should be hitting them in the pocket, we should be focusing on the blackout days when we don't spend money. But, you know, I feel like we should do both. And I feel like I support both. And I will tell you why I support both. I support both because when you have a civil unrest like this, there are three types of people in the streets: There are the protesters, there are the rioters and there are the looters. The protesters are there because they actually care about what is happening in the community, they want to raise their voices and they're there strictly to protest. You have the rioters, who are angry, who are anarchists, who really just want to fuck shit up, and that is what they are going to do regardless. And then you have the looters. And the looters almost exclusively are just there to do that: to loot. And now, people are like, "What did you gain?" "What did you get from looting?"

I think that as long as we are focusing on the what, we're not focusing on the why, and that is my issue with that. As long as we are focusing on what they are doing, we are not focusing on why they are doing. Some people are like, "Well, those aren't people who are legitimately angry about what's happening. Those are people who just want to get stuff." Okay, well then, let's go with that; let's say that's what it is. Let's ask ourselves why, in this country, in 2020, the financial gap between poor Blacks and the rest of world is at such a distance that people feel like that their only hope and only opportunity to get some of the things that we flaunt and flash in front of them all the time is to walk through a broken glass window and get it. They are so hopeless that getting that necklace, getting that TV, getting that change, getting that bag, getting that phone, whatever it is that they are going to get, is that in that moment when the riots happen and they are presented with an opportunity of looting, that is their only opportunity to get it. We need to be questioning that why. Why are people that poor? Why are people that broke? Why are people that food insecure? That clothing insecure? That they feel like their only shot—that they're shooting their shot by walking through a broken glass window to get what they need. And then people want to talk about, "Well, there are plenty of people who pulled themselves up by their bootstraps and got it on their own. Why can't they do that?"

Let me explain something about economics in America. (And I'm so glad that as a child I got an opportunity to spend time at PUSH, where they taught me this.) It's that we must never forget that economics was the reason that Black people were brought to this country. We came to do the agricultural work in the South and the textile work in the North. Do you understand that? That is what we came to do. We came to do the agricultural work in the South and the textile work in the North. Now, if I right now—if I right now decided that I wanted to play Monopoly with you, and for four hundred rounds of playing Monopoly, I didn't allow you to have any money. I didn't allow you to have anything on the board. I didn't allow for you to have anything, and then we played another fifty rounds of Monopoly, and everything that you gained and you earned while you were playing that round of Monopoly was taken from you. That was Tulsa. That was Rosewood. Those are places where we built Black economic wealth. Where we were self-sufficient. Where we owned our stores. Where we owned our property. And they burned them to the ground. So that's four hundred and fifty years, so for four hundred rounds of Monopoly, you don't get to play at all. Not only do you not get to play; you have to play on the behalf of the person that you're playing against. You have to play and make money and earn wealth for them, and then you have to turn it over to them. So then for fifty years you finally get a little bit, and you're allowed to play, and every time that they don't like the way that you're playing or that you're catching up or that you're doing something to be self-sufficient, they burn your game. They burn your cards. They burn your Monopoly money. And then, finally, after release and the onset of that, they allow you to play, and they say, "Okay, now you catch up." At this point the only way you're going to catch up in the game is if the person shares the wealth. Correct? But what if every time you share the wealth, then there is psychological warfare against you to say: "Oh, you're an equal opportunity hire."

So, if I play four hundred rounds of Monopoly with you, and I had to play and give you every dime that I made, and then for fifty years every time that I played and if you didn't like what I did, you got to burn like they did in Tulsa and like they did in Rosewood. How can you win? How can you win? You can't win. The game is fixed. So when they say, "Why do you burn down the community? Why burn down your own neighborhood?" It's not ours! We don't *own* anything! We don't own *anything*! There is . . . Trevor Noah said it so beautifully last night. There is a social contract that we all have that if you steal or if I steal, then the person who is the authority comes in, and they fix the situation. But that the person that fixes this situation is killing us! So the social contract is broken! And if the social contract is broken, why the fuck do I give a shit about burning the fucking Football Hall of Fame or about burning a fucking Target? You broke the contract when you killed us in the street and didn't give a fuck! You broke the contract when for four hundred years, we played your game and built your wealth! You broke the contract when we built our wealth again on our own, on our bootstraps in Tulsa, and you dropped bombs on us! When we built it in Rosewood and you came in and you slaughtered us! You broke the contract! So fuck your Target! Fuck your Hall of Fame! As far as I'm concerned, they could burn this bitch to the ground. And it still wouldn't be enough. And they are lucky that what Black people are looking for is equality and not revenge.

As soon as the last word came out of my mouth, I broke down. I felt a sense of relief as if the weight of carrying that message had been lifted and the only thing left was to cry out any remnants of the pain attached to it. My dear friend Brandi was

off to the side wearing a matching George Floyd tee and immediately opened her arms to receive me. When I was talking
about the social contract being broken, I was referring to something Trevor Noah had said on *The Daily Show* a few nights
before. He was talking about the way white people weapon-
ize and leverage whiteness against us. He said that they were
breaking the social contract that is supposed to keep the society
organized: we don't hurt each other, and when someone does,
society has a remedy to address the harm. The police killing of
George Floyd, a man who wasn't even accused of a violent act,
breaks the social contract. The Civil Rights Movement of the
1960s was our attempt to get this country to extend the social
contract to us. To at least treat us with the same respect they
insist on for themselves. Under the Atlanta sun, days into a protest that would rock the world, reality as I knew it ran smack
into some people's delusions, and I told the truth. Stronger
people than me have gone off, with much less provocation.

There are moments when a force that's bigger than you takes
over, and this was a moment like that for me. I was mad, and the
history I knew, the ideas I'd been teaching, and the presence of
ancestors who had a lot to say, moved through me, weaving it
all together with a clarity and power as big as my anger. I'm not
sure I was in control of what came out of my mouth, but I do
think it was more eloquent and truer than what I might have
said if I had given it more thought. I knew I had spoken the
truth. I just didn't know what it might cost me.

When David posted the video, I was nervous. But at the
same time, I felt like Black protesters and political commentators
had been talking around the most important aspects of George
Floyd's murder and the uprising in response. I hadn't planned to
say what I said, but I managed to say everything I felt needed to

be said: we were risking our lives to protest during a pandemic because the deaths of Black people reminded us that in America, we are not promised another day, even if we do everything right. Breonna Taylor was a model citizen. She was asleep in her bed when she was killed. We are not safe no matter what we do. And the other thing, particularly in light of the looting, was that, NO!, we don't think property is equal to or more important than our precious, fragile lives. And really, how dare anyone act as though the insured property and inventory of a multimillion-dollar corporation is more valuable than we are. That is the voice of slave masters trying to tell us who we are. But we are not slaves. I'm not making a case for looting, but as I said in the video, why are people so food and clothing insecure that this is the only way they can imagine having what they need? Not want, need. When I hear people talking about rioting and looting, my response is: replace those words with "Dead Black People." See which one hits harder. Martin Luther King Jr. said, "A riot is the language of the unheard." America, I ask you, what have you failed to hear? What are you studiously ignoring?

After the video went live on YouTube, I expected to be canceled. *I'm Not Dying with You Tonight*, the YA book I cowrote with my friend Gilly Segal, had been out for a year, and it had even been nominated for an NAACP Image Award. I was sure our publisher was going to cancel our contract for a second book. I thought my writing career was over. Even with all the experience I have, working in TV and on movies, I thought I might be canceled there too. But at the same time, as an activist who has worked in my community for years (I was fighting food insecurity when I was an eleven-year-old using my allowance to feed homeless people in Chicago), I felt it was important to stand for the truth as I see it too.

I've never kept my opinions to myself when I've thought there was something worth saying. My mother liked to tell a story—she calls it the first time I went viral—about taking my sister and me to Washington, DC, when I was in middle school. While we were sightseeing, a news crew asked Angie for her thoughts on the conflict with Iran. Having plenty of opinions about US foreign policy, I interrupted to add to what Angie said and ended up taking the mic and giving President Reagan some advice. For days after, my mother was deluged with friends and relatives calling to make sure that was really me on the evening news.

Once, when I was in high school, I was riding on the train with my girlfriends, and an older woman stepped on the train, a few stops before the red line separated the North Side from the South Side of Chicago. She glared at us. "Why do you have to be so loud?" In all honesty our colorful train performance may have been a bit much for tired workers on a weekday afternoon. I think I was shocked because I had thankfully never been told to tone it down prior to this moment. My mom acknowledged very early on that I was going to be nothing short of a loud woman. She allowed me to own that and put me in environments where it was okay to express myself. When I talk to loud women and girls who tell me that growing up their big voices were frowned upon, we discuss how the narrative is spun against them to give voice to quieter ladies. It's so unnecessary. You do not have to mute one group to create space for another.

That lady on the train all those years ago certainly missed out on an interesting trio. Tanji Harper is now the artistic director of the Happiness Club, a Chicago-based organization designed to encourage positive values and social change through the arts, and was honored in 2018 by the Obama Foundation. Leigh Peeler just finished a run as Deloris Van Cartier, the lead in *Sister Act*, the musical, with the Charleston Light Opera Guild. And then there was me.

After my video went viral, internationally, I saw many people saying they couldn't get past how I delivered my message. If you attempt to judge a larger-than-life queen, you may miss your chance to encounter a glorious peacock. The people who tried to dismiss me as a loud, ghetto, angry Black woman did not see an award-winning filmmaker, community advocate and successful YA author. They could not wrap their minds around the notion that a hood girl could be a hero too.

In this day and age, there is still something intimidating about Black women who don't code switch, have an opinion and own booming voices dripping with phrases that are unapologetically rooted in hip-hop culture. To clarify, the way we speak is cultural, not remedial. The question should never be "Do women like me deserve a voice in the world?" Obviously, we do. Black girls who come from nothing have been the architects of cool since the turn of the twentieth century. This is why I was proud to be the voice of the voiceless. I'm not saying we should make noise for noise's sake. I'm just saying no one should tell us to shut up.

As the hours went by, I began to see responses across Twitter, Instagram, Facebook and on YouTube. There were a few negatives:

The establishment don't really cares what you have to say . . . Sorry good try though . . .

My dear-thank you for the truth-please next time you go public—please make your hair a different hairstyle—)to present your face(, wishing the Black civilization a great future).

But the comments were overwhelmingly positive:

My God! As a Black woman here in the u.s. she is speaking FOR my soul's pain! Tears are in my eyes, from hearing someone so eloquently put the distilled simple truth of all Black people's reality in this country! Thank you sis!

Hi, I've just finished watching this video of Kimberly here (first time hearing her speak): I started off thinking "yeah, it's good" and finished it with "holy shit, wow."

Her ability to be able to drive the point home with the emotion . . . just really powerful. I shared it with my girlfriend who said it made her cry a little.

If this video don't make you see a clearer picture of what's going on and why. Then you will stay sleep. Well said young Lady. I get chills every time I watch this.

Best explanation ever. There will never be equality. They want Black people to help them protect what they stole from them in the first place.

👏👏👏👏👋👋👋yas my Sista you are speaking FACTS !!!! Every word you said touched my spirit

I cried for the first time in 45 yrs. . . . I strongly share all sentiments sister. . . . Keep on educating us. . . .

Damn!!!! "They are lucky, that what Black people are looking for is equality and not revenge!!!!" What a powerful line.

This needs to be in schools.

I felt the spirit of the ancestors rising with this one

LeBron James tweeted:

I'm Here For You

I never expected the outpouring of support I received from
all over the world. It turned out that people understood what
I was saying and felt it was what they also wanted to say but
didn't know how. Suddenly, I was making appearances on
late-night talk shows in the US, Europe and Australia. I was
in conversation with Black members of parliament in the UK.
In Belgium, there's a 44-meter (144-foot) wide mural with the
word "EQUALITY" and a quote of mine from the video. I was
even *GQ Germany*'s 2020 Voice of the Year. It's a surprise to
find the world listening to this educated yet socially unpol-
ished Black woman from the South Side of Chicago by way of
Atlanta, Georgia. I didn't expect the world to be ready for my
long, bedazzled nails, colorful and ever-changing hair choices
and masterful command of whatever the latest slang is. I have
used this to my advantage as I travel the country with my
organization, The People's Uprising, where I serve as the enter-
tainment and culture chair. I have always had something to say.
I just haven't always had the world ready to listen.

HOOD GIRLS CAN BE HEROES TOO

One of the things one must consider about being Black in America is how LUCKY any of us has to be to get to adulthood without so much trauma and so many scars we can barely function. I'm a Black person who grew up here, so, of course, I have some scars, but I got lucky in a few different ways.

I was raised on the South Side of Chicago, the youngest of seven. After my parents divorced, my mom, who had four kids, married my stepdad, who had three kids, so we were Chicago's Brady Bunch. Not every hood experience is *the* hood experience. I grew up in a two-parent home and both of my parents worked. What was happening inside my house combated what was happening outside. The neighborhood where I grew up was eight blocks of working- and middle-class families, but it was boxed in by the hood. Go three or four blocks in any direction and you'd be in gang territory. It was the mid-1980s, and drugs were everywhere. Now when people talk about neighborhood violence, it's a shock to realize how much more violent Chicago was when I was a kid. I think you could say the same about any big American city. On one hand, I witnessed my first murder at fifteen. On the other, the hood armed me with a lot of skills I use every day.

When you're the baby in a big family, you learn how to fight and make your voice heard, and that's been working pretty well for me lately. You also get to learn a lot about the world being surrounded by folks who are older and figuring stuff out for themselves. Since she was an activist, my mother was friends with a lot of politicians, so I ear hustled a lot of conversations about what was going on in the world and Black people's situation. I was raised to really love and stand up for Black people. All of that stuck with me. I had a lot of great role models and people invested in me. I was always a creative kid, and my mother nurtured that every way she could. When I wanted to rap, my mother made sure me and my little crew had T-shirts for our "look." When I decided I wanted to go into theater, she found every drama program she could. Growing up where I grew up, if your kids show interest in anything, you jump on that to keep them out of trouble. My mom was really committed to making sure we had some experiences and education and some tools that gave us a big sense of who we could be in our lives. So that was my luck. And until I got to high school, I was lucky with teachers too.

By high school, I became . . . problematic. I was a rabble-rouser as a teenager, but as an adult, I think maybe I was just sensitive about being in spaces where I wasn't welcome. I went to three high schools. Years later, I was diagnosed as having ADHD, and I think not knowing that made everything worse, but the first school I went to—Mother McAuley, in Chicago— was a miserable, racist nightmare. The parochial school was a

PWI (predominantly white institution), and I was one of the very few Black kids there. At McAuley, I got called "nigger" like it was a punctuation. Someone put a noose on my locker. It was the '90s, but that place was deep into the white supremacist delusion, and it just brutalized me. It felt like I was going to fight a war every day. Just to go to school.

I finally left Mother McAuley when this white girl, sitting behind me in class, cut my hair. Given the cloth I was cut from, growing up where I grew up, I did what I knew to do, which was to beat her ass. After that, those girls had a target on my back, and it got so bad that I ran away from home. My sister, who is six years older than me, was in college at Purdue, so I took the Greyhound to visit her and refused to come home until my parents found me a new school.

It was the middle of the year, so my mom had no choice but to put me in Julian, the local public high school. I went from one type of brutalization to another. The school was having real issues with fighting and gangs. Julian had metal detectors before other schools. But even with all that, I still felt safer than I did with the racist white kids. My parents had a little more money than most, and I had nice clothes. My mother grew up being picked on because of her clothes, so she put name brands on her children every day. When I got to Julian, ten girls jumped me and took everything. Even my shoes. The most humiliating part was how quickly word spread through my neighborhood about me getting jumped. At school, I kept my head down and mostly stayed to myself after that, but in my neighborhood, it was after this moment that I ceased getting bullied and became more fearless and learned how to stand up for myself. Unfortunately, in my neighborhood that meant learning how to fight. Even more unfortunate was becoming comfortable with violence as an answer. I'm nothing like that today, and this is where the problem of villainizing children is a danger. It's criminal for adults to villainize sixteen-year-olds—like Ma'Khia Bryant, who was gunned down by a cop—because we have no way of knowing what's on the other side. Consider teenage cigarette-smoking Barack Obama. Resources can turn that life around.

Having been in both those environments, one of the things I think about now is how easy it is to decide about a kid—as if who they are at fourteen or sixteen or nine is who they are always going to be. I was a terrible kid when I was unhappy and in pain and it didn't feel like any place would be good for me. And shout-out to my mom for not just surviving my teenage years but helping me to find a good place. But I think it's important to say that Jay-Z was a bad kid. Biggie Smalls was a bad kid. Look at a kid like Trayvon Martin—who they criminalized— and wonder what he could have been. People thought I was a bad kid. There are judges who were bad kids. We don't know who people will grow up to be. We don't know what they have inside them or what they can offer to this world. White kids get the benefit of the doubt, but Black kids don't. When you have a Dylann Roof that shoots up a church and kills nine people, he's a "troubled" kid. He's a mass murderer, and the language people use makes it sound like he just needs a little help. But they'll call Trayvon Martin a thug. I would like to see that change.

I was at Julian until the end of sophomore year. Sophomore year, I was heading back from homecoming and watched one of my homeboys get beaten to death. In this era, we went to funerals like it was going to the club. It was the height of the drug trade, and gangs were always beefing about territory. My friend, who I'll call Sweet, was the one who was killed. We were coming home from the dance, and we knew our friend was at the edge of a territory he didn't belong in. We told him not to walk us home, and then, before he could leave, he was spotted by a guy who recognized him. That guy did this kind of whistle, and all these guys came out of nowhere. They had bats and clubs, and they just beat Sweet to death. My friends and I were in prom dresses running into the street, trying to flag down cars. Trying to save Sweet. The code of the street was those guys weren't going to hit girls, so they were pushing us to get away from him. Finally, this guy stopped, pulled over, drew his AR and let out a warning shot. Those boys all ran away, leaving Sweet on the sidewalk. Me and my friends sat on either side of him and held him until the ambulance came, but he was already gone. I walked home with blood on my dress.

The thing to understand about that moment is even though I was burying my friends, gangs and the way we lived in that world was our normal. A lot of the guys in our neighborhood joined gangs because of the camaraderie. It's second nature in Chicago, and it's not viewed as a bad thing. A gang is a family of guys who have pretty cars and girls, and back then Chicago gangs were exceptionally organized. You can't operate as an independent drug dealer. That would get you killed.

For the guys who join, they don't get exposed to any other way out. The people they see working regular jobs look sad to them. You see a guy working as a mechanic in the day and as a security guard at night. And he's probably scraping, making barely enough money to keep it together. Then you see a guy who pulls up in a brand-new Benz and the cutest girl in the neighborhood.

We can't be surprised when gang life makes more sense to a young guy. We don't trust wealth unless it's owned and tangible. Gang wealth is in the clothes and the cars. When gangster Flukey Stokes's twenty-eight-year-old son, Willie "The Wimp," was shot and killed, his funeral was featured in *Jet* magazine. He was buried sitting up in a coffin made to look like a Cadillac. That's a show of wealth, if that's what you know. Flukey Stokes had so much money his son got a new Cadillac every year, and his family could afford to bury a perfectly good front grille and trunk, just so his son could go in style.

I've only recently recognized how moments like seeing Sweet die and going to all those funerals traumatized me. Even though I had the benefits of growing up with some privilege, I was exposed to a lot. Violence was so commonplace in Chicago that it didn't register as traumatic.

Sophomore year I also had an amazing English teacher. She was teaching Shakespeare, and I was so interested and involved. She pulled my mother aside and said, "Your daughter is bright and gifted, and she shouldn't be here. You have to find her someplace else to go." So we started looking for another place for me to go, and I ended up at the Chicago Academy for the Arts. It was like I'd arrived on the island of misfit toys and found my squad.

Chicago Academy for the Arts was a safe haven for me. It was culturally diverse, and racially, it was pretty evenly mixed. And we were all artists, so we had all been outsiders wherever we came from. Because the school was small—there were twenty-five people in my graduating class—we were very close, and we defended and protected each other. I've been using my hair as a political statement since I was in high school. In my neighborhood, people thought I was weird, but at school, there were fifty other kids with expressive hair. Mother McAuley was an experience of the kinds of attacks a lot of Brown girls face, but the arts school was a healing, happy place for me.

Being at the Chicago Academy for the Arts set my path for life. For years I thought I would be a professional rapper, and I performed with a few hip-hop crews while attending Julian and later when I moved to LA. I always knew I would do creative work. Art is the best portal I know to enter difficult conversations. There are so many ways we resist seeing each other, but through art, we find new ways to encounter different perspectives. Being part of the first generation to grow up with hip-hop, its values have informed my understanding of the role of art. If hip-hop is the news, always reflective of its moment, I want all of the artistic work I do to meet that standard. I went to film school, but it wasn't a good fit. From this vantage point, I can see that I learn best by doing, and the work I had the good fortune to do in Los Angeles and Atlanta was the real film education I needed.

Sometimes people get lost trying to figure out who they are. When you're the baby in a big family, you learn early to assert yourself and make your voice heard. I always knew who I was. My path was twofold, trying to find a world where I could be that person, and trying to find the best artistic expression for my ideas and what is important to me. That search took me to many places, including studying circus arts at the Ringling Brothers Clown College. Today people often describe me as fearless. If I'm fearless as an activist, it's because I was willing to try a lot of new things and follow some unusual paths to know what I'm made of. I'm fearless as an activist because my choices made me fearless as a person. I won't pretend it was an easy road. I was a prize fighter. I broke my hand during my first fight and still kept fighting and winning. I've had some wonderful highs in my life, but the low moments were pretty desperate. That said, even some of the lowest moments eventually took me to places I needed to be.

At one point, when my son was still little, I hit rock bottom. I had fallen apart. I was in Atlanta, which meant I wasn't going to be homeless because I had enough family around, but here I was, as an adult, and I was so much more impoverished than I had been as a child. I had dedicated myself to my career as an artist and worked so hard, but I hadn't graduated from college, and there weren't a lot of jobs I could get. And now I was broke, and I was the mother of a young child. For the first two years of his life my son and I lived in a house without gas, so we didn't have hot water. I could afford to pay the electric bill but I couldn't pay the gas bill too. To bathe him and to bathe myself I boiled water on a space heater and we stayed in one room to keep warm.

It's expensive to be broke. Not only is it expensive, it's humiliating. When you go to get the services you need, people treat you like you are trash. They have no respect for your time. I'd have to give up an entire day to pick up food stamps. The sentiment is "What do you care, you're not working." The message is "You ain't shit. Your time is not valuable." Now people completely value my time. But when I was poor they decided my time was valueless. And when you are poor people decide your life is valueless.

In Georgia, to get food stamps and Temporary Assistance for Needy Families (TANF), you have to go through a career education program. During the first month, they help you do a résumé, and part of what you have to do is show up for a session in professional clothing. They give you a gas card or a MARTA (public transportation) card, and you are supposed to go out and apply for jobs. It's so humiliating. They give you a paper you have to take with you and get the manager at each location to sign the paper as proof that you applied. Who is going to hire you if they know you are going to apply for welfare? This kind of resistance to hiring is faced by the formerly incarcerated too.

I came upon the bookstore Little Shop of Stories. They had story time and different events for kids, and I thought this would be a great place for my son. I applied for a job but didn't put it on the list or ask them to sign my form because I really wanted to put my best foot forward and didn't want to play myself out of the position. They called me the next day for a job interview. I went in on a Thursday, and they said I could start on Monday. I never got TANF because I got that job. I started at Little Shop of Stories in 2010. I had not been involved with anything related to books in over a decade. When I left the poetry scene and stopped doing spoken-word competitions, I had thrown all my energy into pursuing filmmaking.

Little Shop of Stories was a great place for me to be. I read lots of books and got to see the power of kid lit (children's literature) and YA (young adult) writing. At the bookstore, I started moderating panels of kid lit and attending events at national conferences. Then my friend Gilly and I sold a book idea. It took us two and a half years to write it.

Working at the bookstore was the gateway to a lot of fantastic experiences. Once, when I was working at Little Shop of Stories, I went to the home of children's book writer and illustrator Anita Lobel. She's a World War II concentration camp survivor, and she was telling me about her experience. I mentioned that my uncle John, my stepdad's brother, served in the 761st Tank Battalion with Jackie Robinson. The 761st was the terrestrial equivalent of the Tuskegee Airmen. The members of the battalion stayed friends for life, and, being proud of Uncle John, I was talking about how the 761st was one of the units in the Battle of the Bulge when Ms. Lobel began to cry. I thought I had offended her, so I was busy apologizing when she explained that the soldiers from the 761st liberated the camps because the high command knew that when the survivors saw Black men, they would immediately understand them to be the Americans.

Since I grew up hearing Uncle John's stories, I knew that Jackie Robinson had been a second lieutenant in the battalion. When Robinson refused to move to the back of a military shuttle bus in Camp Hood, Texas, they tried to court-martial him. But the unit had to sign off on the court-martial, and they wouldn't do it. Those guys really had each other's backs, and I got to see that in the way they kept up with each other, long after the war was over. When I think about how this exceptional group of men changed their own lives and their perceptions of what Black people could do, I'm amazed by how much that just reverberated out in waves to all the folks they touched, whatever they did after the war.

Talking with Anita Lobel, I realized that it was just another example of how we touch so many people and change the world in so many positive ways but haven't been able to reap the benefits of our labor. Those men came home and were not able to participate in the GI Bill in the same way their white counterparts were

able. They were not able to get the home loans for homeownership and other benefits that white men enjoyed.

I wasn't always a big reader, but when I was ten years old, I
spent the summer in rural Illinois at my grandmother's farm and
found a Scholastic book about a girl who is forced to go on a
cruise with her grandma and ends up meeting a cute boy. I just
fell in love with it. Prior to that I had never really read a story
that had kids as the protagonists. I read that book over and over
and by the end of the summer, I was a reader, just looking for
books to fall in love with. My next love match was *Manchild in
the Promised Land* by Claude Brown. My eighth grade assigned
Manchild, and even though the main character was male, I
related to it. It's written in AAVE (African American Vernacular English), and the story reminded me of boys I was growing
up with who were in and out of juvenile detention. But this
is the real magic of stories. Even though it wasn't my life, I
could still see myself on the page. The power of the language
and the representation in *Manchild* was part of my decision to
write the character of Lena in my book *I'm Not Dying with You
Tonight* in AAVE. I knew the power of reading yourself.

The other part of that decision came from working at the
Little Shop of Stories. When I worked there, we participated in
Project Bookshelf, a program where kids who were in the free
or reduced lunch program would come in before every school
break to get free books. I would recommend fantastic books
to them, but they would take them home and not read them.
Finally, I found a book called *Cookie: A Fort Worth Story*. It was
a story, written in AAVE, about a young girl whose circumstance the kids could relate to, and they loved it. Just seeing

how they responded to Cookie reminded me of how hungry I had been as a kid to read anyone who was writing about the world I knew. It made me committed to being a mirror for those girls.

Another program we had at Little Shop of Stories was On the Same Page, a community-wide read in which kids who got assistance could get the book we were reading for free. So many of the kids told the two women that ran the program that the first books they owned were the books they got from On the Same Page. It made me grateful for my lived experience in which a book was the only thing my mother would never say no to. Both of my parents are readers, and being a reader, loving stories and having books as a gateway to other worlds has been immensely important to my own life. From the Little Shop of Stories, to writing, to working with children's literature with the Library of Congress, I have worked with multiple communities and organizations to enlarge the love of reading and access to books.

In 2015, my good friend Gilly Segal saw a new clip about the unrest in Baltimore after the death of Freddie Gray in police custody. The news story was about how the administration at Frederick Douglass High School found out about the protest and sent the kids home early. But the police and everybody had already shut down public transportation, and that's how most of those kids get home. So the kids got trapped behind a police barricade. But the news didn't care about that. It was just a fact mentioned in passing as part of a longer story. Nobody circled back. She and I searched around and couldn't find out what happened to those kids. We're both moms, so we were worried about what became of those babies.

Gilly had the idea to write a story about some kids trying to survive the night. But, as a white woman, she was clear that it wasn't her voice or her lived experience, so she asked if I would be interested in writing the novel together. We came up with the idea to set the story in Atlanta, because it's our city, and have two girls trying to survive the night. I would write Lena, the Black girl's voice, and Gilly would write Campbell, the white girl's voice, to show how differently they see the same events based on the differences in their lived experiences. Later, in the summer of 2020, when the uprising in Atlanta began and unfolded in pretty much the way Gilly and I had imagined in our book, *I'm Not Dying with You Tonight* looked more like prophesy than fiction.

I'm Not Dying with You Tonight became a *New York Times* best seller, and was nominated for the NAACP Image Award for Outstanding Literary Work: Youth/Teens. I'm really proud of the footprint the book has made, but I'm even prouder of all the calls I've received from teachers saying, "I couldn't get my kids to read anything this year, but they read *I'm Not Dying with You Tonight*. Will you please come talk to my school?" Gilly and I ended up having to do two national tours to cover just a third of the schools that asked us to come. And unlike most authors, we primarily went to Title I schools, and we made sure those kids had the books free of charge when we got there.

Even with the success of the book, some Black people have rejected the choice I made to write Lena's voice in AAVE, but I knew who I was writing for. I was writing for me as a kid, and I was writing for all the girls I was trying to inspire to read when I was at Little Shop of Stories. I started #hoodgirlscanbeheroestoo because when you're a hood chick, you're being told at every turn that the way you are is unacceptable. I always say that the way I speak is cultural, not remedial. I can code switch as well as anyone, but I am not willing to believe my home code is a liability. Black people have spent too long trying to serve the losing game of respectability politics, at the expense of appreciating the genius of our culture.

Hood girls are the architects of cool. We teach everybody what's hip and happening. If you talk about language or style, it all comes from hood girls and trans girls. Hood girls and trans girls teach everybody how to be. How to live. How to do. And as we're inventing it, people dismiss us. They call us ignorant and dumb, but in a month, somebody's going to be packaging and monetizing every word we used. All the vernacular that white suburban kids are using this year, we were done with three years ago. And people have the nerve to call us ignorant.

By making Lena the hero of *I'm Not Dying with You Tonight*, the girls who saw themselves on the page could also see that the survival skills they use, and the way they know how to read a situation, made them more capable of navigating the unexpected and keeping themselves safe. They could read *I'm Not Dying with You Tonight* and see themselves as heroes. When we were on our book tour, we would get to a school, and the girls would have made stickers or a banner that said, "Hood Girls Can Be Heroes Too." They were so excited to get that recognition and to show me that they got it. I know a hood girl is brilliant and magical. I'm committed to that vision, so I'm riding with hood girls forever.

FOUR HUNDRED ROUNDS OF MONOPOLY

From where I stand, the COVID-19 pandemic turned out to be the game changer that opened the world to conversations everyone had been ignoring. In our regular, daily lives, we move too fast. We have so much mental stimuli—from work, relationships, obligations, etc.—that we don't have the time or the space to just sit down and process the world we live in and how we feel about it. But during the pandemic, we sat still. We weren't glued to our phones. For many of us, there was less active stress, and we could finally let the world in. So when we had the back-to-back deaths of Breonna Taylor, Ahmaud Arbery and George Floyd, and we were at home feeling the world, instead of thinking about it and dismissing what we didn't have the emotional space for, the brutality of Derek Chauvin kneeling on George Floyd's neck for nine minutes and twenty-nine seconds broke us. On another day, in another year, when we weren't worried about COVID-19 and feeling like our elderly and sick relatives might die from a virus before we could see them again, we might have shaken off each new death the way we've grown accustomed to doing. But in 2020, uniquely, every death was a personal wound to us, and we couldn't escape the pain of them. And everything that happened next, as people risked their lives to take to the street because they simply could not let these deaths go unmarked and unpunished, is what it looks like when we finally wake up and speak our pain.

It may be too early to say that America is forever changed. The way the global civil unrest of 2020 focused our attention on the long-overdue conversations this country needs to have is progress. In the 1960s, the Civil Rights Movement (I include every version of resistance in this, from Martin Luther King Jr. to the Black Panthers and the Nation of Islam) fought for Black people to be treated equally in this country. Their fight changed America and our situation in many important ways. But it didn't erase the history. In fact, in many ways it tiptoed around America's worst offenses and put Band-Aids on the bloodiest wounds. That was then. Now, we are fighting for nothing less than the dismantling of the historically racist systems that have been brutalizing Black and Brown people since the founding of the nation. We know we're equal to white people. Only a person in the deepest throes of the white supremacist delusion would say we aren't. But now we're fighting for equity. And we won't get to equity until we rethink the system from the ground up.

The first line of what I say in the video is part of a speech I heard as a child. As a kid in Chicago, I was the youngest of seven kids, and my parents' way to keep us all on track was by making sure we stayed busy with a lot of after-school programs. I spent a lot of time at the DuSable Museum of African American History and at the Operation PUSH/Rainbow Coalition after school. At PUSH/Rainbow, there was a wonderful woman, the Reverend Willie T. Barrow, who led the kids' program. Reverend

Barrow was an awesome woman known by most people in Chicago for her activism and organizing—she marched with Martin Luther King Jr. and worked with everyone from Jesse Jackson to Barack Obama. As children, she taught us about the economics of Black America. And she taught us that there is a through line between what happened during Reconstruction—the period after slavery—and the way white people, Southerners especially, dismantled Reconstruction with the creation of the Jim Crow system. She explained the unbroken line between Jim Crow and the mass incarceration, voter disenfranchisement and inequity we are still dealing with today. Once, when I was about eleven years old, she gave a lecture about the economics of slavery and its ripple effects.

It began: "We must never forget that economics was the reason Black people were brought to America. We did not arrive on America's shores like other immigrants, looking for freedom and the land of opportunity. We came to make others rich. We came to do the work that others could, or would not, do. The slave was the backbone of the agricultural economy in the South and the textile industry in the North." Even as a kid, that speech made so many things clear to me.

When I was in eighth grade, my teacher put me in an oratory contest, and I showed her the transcript of Reverend Barrow's speech that I got from the *Chicago Defender*. I used that speech for many oratory competitions, so in June 2020, it was already deep in me, and I had been thinking about the implications of the information in that speech for decades. As I read our history or saw the inequities and injustices we deal with, I always had Reverend Barrow's speech to help me organize what I was taking in. If you're Black, you don't have to look far to see economic disenfranchisement and the ways we live at a disadvantage in this country. I could see all of that just walking around my own neighborhood.

I guess it was natural that on that day in downtown Atlanta, when David turned his camera on me, the first thing out of my mouth would be Reverend Barrow's wisdom, *"We must never forget that economics was the reason Black people were brought to America."* And everything I said after represented all the ways I'd been thinking about our position in this country, framed by the words of her speech thirty years before.

That should also be a note to parents. We have to be very conscious and careful about what we're implanting in our kids because those things stay. They stick, and you don't know where or when they'll bear fruit. I was blessed that that's the kind of stuff that was implanted in me. As parents, as aunties and uncles, we have to stay aware of the kids in our lives and offer them the lessons and ideas that nurture them and have the potential to grow within them.

Here's another example: when I was a kid and my mother had errands to do on a Saturday, she would send us to the Carter G. Woodson library to hang out. We would walk around and explore, or just find a good spot to read in. I love that library. It's known for its large African American studies collection and it's one of my happy places. Even now, just spending some time there can cheer me up. I was about eighteen, when I was browsing and came across a book about massacres in the United States. I opened it up and read about the 1921 race massacre in Tulsa for the very first time. I learned about Dick Rowland, a Black nineteen-year-old who had been accused of assaulting a white elevator operator named Sarah Page (the Oklahoma Historical Society says that she likely screamed when Rowland accidentally stepped on her foot after entering the elevator). The men of the Greenwood section of Tulsa, many of whom had served in WWI, went to protect Rowland, showing up at the courthouse to protect the young man from being lynched. This was just two years after the period of terror during which hundreds of Black people were killed with such brutality that James Weldon Johnson, then the executive secretary of the National Association for the Advancement of Colored People (NAACP), called it the "Red Summer."

The next morning, thousands of white people swarmed Greenwood with weaponry, and looted and burned the homes of Greenwood residents, leaving hundreds of dead Black citizens in their wake, many of whom remain unaccounted for, believed by many to be buried in mass graves. Black men were paraded through the streets, arrested—a city gone, and with it, survivors lost homes, property and jobs.

The entry was only a few pages in the book I'd picked up, but I can still recall the feeling of being stunned that something so brutal had happened to Black people, and yet I had never heard of it. Of course, I asked one of the librarians if she had any other books about Tulsa and she showed me titles that focused on the thriving community that created what was known as Black Wall Street.

It was one thing to learn that there had been a race "riot" in which the US government bombed its own citizens. (Many among the mob were deputized by local law enforcement and given firearms.) That was the first shock. But when I read about the success and wealth and Black excellence that had been created and concentrated in this community, it made me furious. A few thousand people had come together to create something extraordinary, not even sixty years after the end of slavery, and they had succeeded. And that community was so thoroughly obliterated that people—including the mentors I could always trust to teach me something or point me in a direction I needed to go to learn something important—didn't even know about it.

I would not have been in the Woodson library learning about Tulsa at eighteen if I hadn't been there hanging out when I was eight. So many of the ways my family organized me as a kid have set my path or guided my curiosity throughout my life. My mother was an activist who worked with kids through many organizations. She was the director of a foster care agency, ran multiple after-school programs and was a counselor with Cradle to Classroom, a program designed to help teen mothers finish school. It was important to her to nurture a love of community in all of her kids, and one of her best-known initiatives was the "Rap Session" event she hosted on Friday nights at Grant Memorial AME church. She basically replicated BET's Teen Summit, a talk show for Black youth that discussed issues guided by professionals in relevant fields. Teens came willingly from all over the city on Friday nights to participate in Rap Session. She made sure we were surrounded by people who cared about the community. She had us volunteering and made sure we knew we were responsible to, and for, the people around us. I'm the baby of my family, my parents had me late in life, and as a child I spent a lot of time with older people.

Long before anyone was "woke," we had a neighbor, Miss Deborah, who was next-level turbo-woke. When I was in middle school, my mother instructed me to wait at Miss Deborah's house until she got home. Miss Deborah would play Dick Gregory tapes for me and talk to me about the Black Panthers. She also was one of the people who cultivated my love of reading, introducing me to some of the writers of Black literature like James Baldwin, Sonia Sanchez and Nikki Giovanni, who I love to this day.

I wish more of us were having the kinds of intergenerational conversations I was lucky enough to have as a kid. A lot of what I talk about—our history, the economics of our situation—is information I first learned from conversations with elders.

There's so much of our history that isn't in the books we read for school. History teachers don't teach our history because they didn't learn it in the schools they went to either. But we are an oral history culture, and our elders have important knowledge to pass on to us, if we're around them and ready to listen. My young experiences with the elders also taught me the value of listening. When someone is talking, I'm not running my counterpoint in my head. People are surprising. We might think we know what someone is about to say, but most of the time, we have no idea. Actually being present to hear what people are telling you, and to ask the questions their words inspire, is one of the best talents I've cultivated. It also helps me slow down when it matters most. Quick and right are not often bedfellows, and I would rather have confidence in the choices I make.

Having adults who were interested in me and always ready to share what they knew with me was a real gift in my life. Now that I have some wisdom, I volunteer with an organization called the Girls Who Brunch Tour. The goal of the organization is to give at-risk girls the tools they need to gain confidence and to become leaders. I teach the girls about finances and economics. So of course, we play Monopoly.

Monopoly wasn't originally imagined as a capitalist game to teach us how to be robber barons. It was designed to teach people how land acquires value and why some pieces of land are more expensive than others. That version, which was created by a white woman named Elizabeth Magie in 1904 and first called the Landlord's Game, would have taught us that the way the value of property can be manipulated creates economic inequality. She was trying to showcase the inequities created when people are allowed to create monopolies. Elizabeth Magie loathed monopolies, and the game was her way to push back against the economic trends that she observed that made acquiring land a game you could only play if you already had a lot of money. She was trying to show how brutal monopolies are to regular working people. Instead, the game we play today teaches us how to consolidate economic power in ways that keep others from thriving. In the original game, there were two sets of rules. One set is close to what we play with today, but in the other rules, wealth is distributed equally. Obviously, that angle was pushed out of the game. The original intention of the game has been lost, but it's still a great way to demonstrate why we, as a nation, have such an enormous wealth gap and how, once you amass enough wealth, you might waste the money, but it's very difficult for anyone to take it from you.

During one of the Girls Who Brunch Tour events, we were playing Monopoly, and as usual, I was talking about the way the game represents building wealth. At some point, one of the girls missed her turn. From that moment, everything about the game went wrong for her. It was only one turn, but she just could not catch up. She was getting frustrated and kept saying, "Miss Kim, can I have two turns in a row? It's not fair because that skipped turn made it so that I couldn't get some stuff that I was supposed to get, and now everybody's catching up." Even though she'd been doing well in the game and was ahead, that one missed turn caused her to fall behind the other players, and even after taking two turns, she couldn't recover. At that moment, it dawned on me that this is what it has been like to be Black in America. You lose so much ground if you miss even one turn, and we have missed so many. Later, after the video was released, I learned that Claud Anderson, who writes and lectures about the economic experience of Black people, also uses Monopoly to explain our situation. Even though our approach and our conversations are different, I appreciated hearing him underline what an apt metaphor Monopoly really is for our situation. It makes sense because Monopoly is itself a metaphor for capitalism, and that is the real game that's been coming for us for four hundred years.

This is the American lie that Black people live every day. Owning real estate is the cornerstone of wealth, and if you don't have the same access to ownership, you can never compete. We live in a system of capitalism, but if you own nothing, capitalism is being done to you, and you have no power. It's significant that every time Black people have begun to thrive, individually or collectively, we have been robbed, beaten and killed to keep us from advancing another step. That's the history of this country. Let's assume that for every Tulsa, Oklahoma, where a whole prosperous community was beaten and bombed out of existence, there were two or three of the same type of wrongs done to smaller communities we don't even know about today. That's been the nature of our experience in this country. When you see the ways in which Black people have been kept from ownership or dispossessed of their land, never imagine our powerlessness is accidental. In our supposedly post-racial society, there are people urging us to catch up, but how could we ever catch up when so much of our labor and earning potential has persistently been suppressed, and they've been building generational wealth for decades?

We cannot talk about money and community economics without first recognizing that wealth is not about the cash you can acquire and save in this lifetime. Money in one lifetime might make you rich, but wealth is the money that endures and grows across generations. It allows a family or an institution to make long-term investments and plans that position it for success but, equally importantly, protect it from failure.

The point I'm making when I talk about four hundred rounds of Monopoly is that the goal of the game is to amass wealth. At every turn of living the game as it's played in the US, we have been denied our turn. Or when we have begun to win, the board has been turned over or set on fire. Four hundred years. Two hundred forty-six years of our ancestors' lives squandered as enslaved people—tools used to build the economy and the wealth of this country. More than one hundred fifty years of playing in systems that have been specifically designed to make sure we are prevented from winning and that keep us from being able to compete. And still, against those odds, some of us have been able to succeed.

There are US companies—Brooks Brothers is an example, but there are plenty more—that began and made their name during slavery. The Brooks Brothers outfitted slaves—the coachmen, the ones who worked in the houses, the ones who greeted people at the door—in tailored clothes. This was how a slave master showed his wealth, by how well-dressed and good-looking his slaves were, particularly his house slaves. Brooks Brothers was founded in 1818, and its ownership was passed down through the Brooks family until it was sold in 1946. Imagine the wealth you could amass for your family if your family business thrived for more than 128 years. In 1818, slaves picked the cotton, so prices were artificially low (because slave labor was not paid for). Brooks Brothers' clothes were sold to slave masters for their slaves, but within 50 years, the company counted Abraham Lincoln as a client. Over 100 years of earning that begins on the backs of slaves and builds generational wealth across centuries. There is no Black person in America that has ever stood in a legacy like that.

We have to name the truth, that where generational wealth was created, there is a generational debt owed to the slaves and servants, and after slavery, the people who were disenfranchised from access to wealth building. In the US, white people have institutions that have endured for centuries because they were allowed to succeed. We have nothing comparable because we were explicitly kept from prospering. So what does that mean today? It means that Brooks Brothers stands on a bedrock of wealth. If a Black person manages to become rich—as a musician or athlete, even as a lawyer or doctor—they are in a very precarious position. If they lose that money, they will not be able to make it back. One bad choice could undo them because they only have the work they can do in this lifetime. That's life without wealth. Uncertain, insecure. It's difficult to make money. It's easy to lose it all.

So we can't be surprised to learn that in 2021, as this book was being written, white people hold 90 percent of the wealth in the US. They are not 90 percent of the population. In fact, they are less than 60 percent of the population. African Americans are just about 14 percent of the population, and yet we only possess 2.6 percent of the wealth. In the US, wealth is most easily and endurably built through homeownership. Between 1925 and 1965, the US government underwrote $200 billion in lending for homeownership. The recipients of all that government money were almost exclusively (98 percent) white people; 2 percent went to nonwhite people—but when I get to the restrictions on where Black people were allowed to live, you'll see that it doesn't make a difference if any of those 2 percent were Black. The government's investment in enrolling white people in homeownership with the offer of low- and no-interest loans created the suburban white middle class as we know it. Millions of working-poor white people became middle class as they took out interest-free government loans and bought subsidized housing.

In those newly created suburbs, the average home price was

$9,000. Choose any suburb you know, go online and look at the value of houses in the area. My bet is those homes cost between $200,000 to $300,000 if you bought one now, depending on where they are. From a $9,000 interest-free investment? Passed down through the generations? Now you understand how wealth is built. A home bought by a family in 1925 and paid off within thirty years has been pure equity—money in the bank—for almost a century. Should I also mention the low cost of college education in this era? This forty-year span from 1925 to 1965 represents the largest affirmative action program the US has ever had. And it was exclusively for white people.

Recently, a friend was telling me about an apartment building a friend of his just bought. It's an old complex, and the original deed said if any Negro stayed in an apartment longer than seventy-two hours, the tenant would be evicted. While whites were encouraged to own homes, in most parts of the US, Black people were not allowed to live outside designated neighborhoods. With the advent of the suburbs, after World War II, homeowners had to agree when they bought their homes that they would not sell to any nonwhite person. In that era, nonwhite could also include Jewish. It most certainly meant Black, Latinx, Native American and Asian. These were laws and covenants that did not get challenged until the 1960s. Even when these restrictions were largely made illegal during the 1980s, banks had already created the policy of redlining Black neighborhoods, so many of the effects persist to this day.

This is why using the game of Monopoly as an analogy makes so much sense. Wealth is built through homeownership and equity. And if you don't have access to either, you are not even in the game. This is important because when you hear white people say we should be pulling ourselves up by our bootstraps, or that their parents did not finish high school but worked hard and were able to offer them the American Dream, they are not acknowledging the truth that the US government gave many of them bootstraps to pull themselves up by, and Black people have never had that. They are the beneficiary of an immense affirmative action program that's designed to deny us. Yes, they are lying to us. But most of all, they are lying to themselves. I don't talk about white supremacy. I talk about the white supremacist delusion. And this—the idea that white people made something of themselves by sheer force of will and hard work—that is the meat of the delusion. Laugh out loud the next time you hear a white person talking crazy like that.

During the push to get white people into homes, the Home Owners' Loan Corporation (HOLC), a government-sponsored bank for mortgage lending, created maps of the US in the 1930s that were coded by income and race. Areas that already had a significant Black and immigrant population appeared on those maps in red as neighborhoods where the HOLC would not lend. We get the term "redlining" from those maps. Understand that Black people had already been localized into spaces where we were uniformly receiving fewer services than the white neighborhoods a few miles away. Then add redlining and the financial certainty that by making investment in our neighborhoods a financial risk, the goods and services available in other neighborhoods wouldn't come to ours. This is the history we have inherited.

This history has many implications, and all of them are bad. Black neighborhoods are consistently undervalued. Take the same house (looks the same, same surface area, same upkeep), put it in a Black neighborhood and its value will be estimated as less than if the same house were in a white neighborhood.

In the eyes of lenders, the presence of Black people lowers the value of the property. The corollary to that piece of injustice is that Black people, on average, are forced to pay higher interest rates on mortgages, regardless of where they buy their home. Black educated professionals pay higher mortgage rates than working-class, uneducated whites, on average. When you add predatory lending practices to the soup, it's easy to see why it has been so difficult for us to even get on the board to play our Monopoly game to build generational wealth. In principle, redlining was made illegal with the Fair Housing Act of 1968, but Black neighborhoods are still undervalued, and Black people still pay more (in mortgage interest) to buy a home.

Unlike most industrialized countries, the US does not educate all children from a national curriculum that offers every child the same education regardless of where they grow up or what their economic circumstance is. Because education in the US is a direct reflection of the taxes paid in the area, if you live in a poor community, the school you go to, paid with taxes from your community, will be under-resourced. So in a neighborhood in which most people own their homes and have, or are building, generational wealth, the tax base from a community of homeowners whose homes are appropriately valued should be enough to fund good schooling. That is not the circumstance of most Black neighborhoods. A report published in 2019 found that in the United States white school districts receive $23 billion more, annually, in annual funds for education than do districts primarily consisting of children of color. Think about that when you see statistics about Black opportunity and success in higher education and high-income professions.

Really think about that: if we live in a Black neighborhood, the enduring effects of redlining will cause us to pay higher interest rates on our mortgage, and higher insurance rates because our neighborhood is considered less safe. And our children will have fewer resources at school and probably not be as well educated as other kids, because the best teachers often want to go where they'll be financially rewarded for their excellence.

The game of Monopoly has been beating our asses since we had the right to choose where we live. This is only the beginning of a conversation about the wealth gap. Regardless of where you are in America, we have not had equal access to any institution or resource. The ways we are organized and the systems we participate in are very different, depending on class and geography. The one constant is wherever we gather in numbers, we get less.

And don't get me started on the cost of the ways white people have appropriated our culture and never paid us a dime. Big Mama Thornton, who wrote and sang the song "Hound Dog" before Elvis Presley stole it, died broke, while his heirs still live in luxury. We have a million and ten stories like that. I'm sure Little Richard would be happy to come back from the grave to talk about the exploitation of Black artists and the theft of Black culture. We have built wealth for so many people and institutions and died hungry.

When you see the big picture, it's easy to understand why Black people are in the economic state that we're in. This is not by happenstance. This is not because Black people are lazy and just don't want to do the work. This is because there have been systems put in place to keep Black people economically disadvantaged. And there have been atrocities that happened repeatedly and went unchecked. In most cases, we did not receive the proper legal response because law enforcement was part of the problem, and the legal system didn't care.

Now that we know where we are, how did we get here?

RECONSTRUCTION

Reconstruction is the historical period after slavery ended (about 1865–1877) and before the start of the Jim Crow period. After the Civil War, the US government enforced the peace by occupying the Southern rebel states. During this period, Black people enjoyed the legal protection of full citizenship, and the government created institutions to assist the more than three million newly freed slaves. The Freedmen's Bureau, led by General Oliver Otis Howard (for whom Howard University, a historically Black college or university [HBCU] in Washington, DC, would later be named), was supposed to help Black people find their way as free Americans. Imagine a few million people who had no idea how to handle money because they had never had any. They had skills but didn't know the value of their labor. And they were vital and necessary to the economy because their labor had been the engine of the South's whole economy, but they had no education, and few had any experience of the world

beyond the plantations where they were enslaved. Ten generations of slaves had been born on US soil, not knowing more
than the experience of slavery.

You've heard people say we never got our forty acres and a
mule? That comes from this period in which Howard, running
the Freedmen's Bureau, gave out allotments of land that had
been confiscated from the white Southerners who fought against
the Union. Howard had about 850,000 acres of confiscated
land, and if he had some mules, he would give you a mule. This
is where the term comes from. He started giving out land, and
Black people started farming the land they had been given. So it
isn't true that we didn't get it. We got it—for a time.

And here's a fun fact: the (derogatory) association between
Black people and watermelon starts during this time. The most
lucrative business that Black people had access to was watermelon
patches. They did not have entrée into cotton and tobacco and
other crops that were big business, but they were allowed to
get seeds to grow watermelons. During Reconstruction when
Black people had big plots of land, a large percentage of them
grew watermelon. Keep in mind that these were people who had
spent their whole lives farming. They knew how to grow food.
Quickly, watermelon sales became synonymous with African
Americans because it was a market they controlled. Newly freed
people made the most of the small opportunity they had and
quickly cornered the market. When white people started calling
African Americans "watermelons" and creating a negative association, it was just their resentment of our community's success.
At a time when few of us could read or write, we still managed
to create thriving businesses. So that's what those of us who got
forty acres did with them. But what's worse than never having

gotten land? Getting the land, pouring our sweat and blood into creating something for ourselves for the very first time and then having the land taken away from us.

When Abraham Lincoln was assassinated, his vice president Andrew Johnson became president of the United States. Johnson had been a poor Southerner, and he felt that the people who received the most horrific treatment in the US were not formerly enslaved people but poor whites. He was not a fan of the rich planter class, and as petty as he was, he used his new position to get back at them. The planters were destitute after the war, and Johnson insisted they come to him to get a personal pardon if they wanted to be given some land to start again. Johnson got to feel like a big man, lording his power over people he didn't like, whom he had felt inferior to for so long. And where was that land coming from? It was the land that had already been given out to formerly enslaved folks. It was the forty acres they were prospering from with watermelon and any other crops they had access to. The land given to former slaves was literally taken back, plot by plot, to be given to white people who had forfeited land in their war against the US.

During Reconstruction, Black men voted for the first time (no women had the vote at that time), and it is estimated that 87 percent of Black men showed up to exercise their rights. Black men become congressmen, and we even had two senators, Hiram Revels and Blanche K. Bruce of Mississippi. The American public education system in the South was created by thirteen Black lawmakers who were in Congress during this period. Black people were political and business leaders. We were thriving and starting new businesses. We were starting towns and using all the skills that used to benefit everyone but us. Keep in mind that these were the people who had been doing all the work, so within these communities, all the necessary skills were represented. There were blacksmiths and carpenters, bakers and midwives. People were leaving plantations where they did all of the work. They may not have had an education, but they were skilled and ready to live free. The ones who could read opened schoolhouses to teach the youth. And we thrived. Which was exactly what former slave owners feared.

All of this was happening at the same time that some of the Southern states responded to the emancipation of former slaves by creating the Black Codes. A loophole in the Thirteenth Amendment (the amendment that outlawed slavery) made slavery illegal EXCEPT as the punishment for a crime. In 1865, South Carolina, Mississippi, Georgia and later Florida enacted laws that made it a crime to NOT work for a white person. And vagrancy was also made a crime. So any Black person who tried to have a farm of their own, or was just standing talking to a friend, could be accused of vagrancy and could get two, three years for that in prison. The Thirteenth Amendment said that nobody else could work for free anymore unless they were incarcerated. So white farmers were in crisis as former slaves left plantations to exercise their rights of free movement, and they used these Black Codes to press Black people back into what was effectively slavery, by accusing them of criminal behavior with every possible excuse. The codes restricted Black property ownership but also the ability to lease land. Freedom of movement was restricted. And if you were convicted of a crime, you would be sent to prison and leased to a plantation to do free work . . . which felt just like slavery. So, depending on where a Black person was, they might be getting some assistance from the Freedmen's Bureau or being pressed back into some new form of slavery.

The Black Codes were (officially) reversed by the Fourteenth Amendment, which gave citizenship to everyone born on US soil, which meant all formerly enslaved people had the full rights of citizenship. In the twelve years between the Emancipation Proclamation, which freed the slaves, and the end of the Reconstruction period in 1877, when the military oversight of the Southern states that had protected Black rights ended, we made extraordinary gains.

In this same time period, after slavery ended, Abraham Lincoln signed the Freedman's Bank Act in 1865 to create a bank for former slaves. This was the only place for Black people to put their money, so the bank grew fast, with thirty-four branches in major cities like Atlanta, Philadelphia and others across the country. Former soldiers had money to deposit, and the Freedman's Bank got all the money Black people were saving as they started businesses and began to find their way. Can you guess what happened next? Fraud and theft. Of course.

In 1871, Congress authorized banks to provide business loans and mortgages, and you already know we didn't see any of that help. But we were diligently trying to build our wealth by saving at the Freedman's Bank. In 1874, when the bank had over sixty thousand Black depositors, it abruptly closed, declared bankruptcy and kept all the money of its depositors, what would be $66 million in today's dollars. The collective wealth of a whole community, across the nation. Gone. Black America was again as destitute as in the immediate aftermath of slavery. But it gets worse. The bank had been managed by white men, and these same white men, mysteriously, suddenly had money to invest in America's newest technology: railroads. They also made questionable loans to friends, and Black America lost everything. An entry on the US Department of the Treasury website quotes Frederick Douglass describing the Freedman's Bank as having been reduced to "the black man's cow but the white man's milk."

The repeating theme of the Black experience in America is the wholesale decimation of our financial potential. This isn't one person, or a few, gambling on a get-rich-quick scheme. This is people believing that the government would never steal from them, at a time when nothing else would have felt safe. The massacres of Black people in Tulsa, Oklahoma, and Rosewood, Florida, are two examples, but this held true for every other place where a whole community was destroyed; all they built was gone in a minute. This is why older Black folks frequently don't trust banks. They are the grandchildren and great-grandchildren of people who were robbed by Freedman's Bank. They are the grandchildren or the children of people who had to grab what they could and run for their lives. And if it wasn't at hand, they would never see it again. If any of you had a grandma who kept her money in the mattress, or in a shoebox at the back of the closet, now you know why. And when Reconstruction ended, the era of Jim Crow began. As has been the way of America, especially in the South, Black people were dragged back to hell.

In the movies when a Black man gets lynched, it's usually a poor person in a one-room house who accidentally did something that angered a white person. The Hollywood version is by no means gospel because in real life the people most likely to be lynched were middle-class or wealthy, land-owning, home-owning, business-owning Black men. And usually, after killing the man white people thought was doing too well, they would burn down his house or his business. The Ku Klux Klan and white militias used lynching as a tool of terror to punish people they saw as troublemakers or who had managed to thrive, against all odds. It was a signal to other Black people that we would not be allowed to do better than them or have more than they had. Terror was a way to isolate people they felt were uppity Negroes who needed to be checked and put in their place. These were preachers and business owners and landholders—the people who were in a position to build generational wealth for their families. The point of killing people who were thriving or challenging white expressions of power and burning their homes and land was to send the message that we would never be allowed to build wealth. And still we tried.

Economist Lisa Cook had the insight that the environmental standards that make the US able to lead in innovation might not hold true for the Black community. Looking at Black inventors and patents filed during Reconstruction, she found that in that unique moment of Black freedom, Black people invented and filed patents at a robust rate. But as Reconstruction ended and the Jim Crow era began, patent filings diminished with each major blow as the legal framework for Jim Crow asserted itself. A key moment when filings, already at a trickle, virtually stopped was 1921, in response to the Tulsa massacre. White mobs had punished a thriving community for its success, and no governmental forces protected it at all.

Based on Dr. Cook's research, it's clear that this moment was the one that made Black people put their heads down, unwilling to risk drawing attention. We had been adding to the wealth of the US economy and contributing to American innovation, and then we stopped. According to Dr. Cook's data, we have still not recovered the high ground we lost, and the US has lost the benefit of more than 1,100 inventions that could have been created by Black inventors if Jim Crow had not convinced them that their intellectual property would not be protected, and they would only be risking their lives. America's racism made us poorer, but it also made the nation poorer. Dr. Cook's estimation of the lost value of those inventions is roughly that of a medium-sized European country in the same time period. Reconstruction was not just the heyday of Black freedom. It was also the peak moment for Black creative agency. This is what we lost when racists were allowed to set the American agenda. This is what we have never recovered.

During the Jim Crow period, Black people effectively had no rights. The Constitution should have protected us, in principle, but it has been well documented that often the same men who policed white communities were some of the same people terrorizing Black communities as members of the Ku Klux Klan, or their local hooded militia. There was no protection for Black people. This was true at the individual level but also for whole communities. During the 1921 so-called race "riot" in Tulsa, Oklahoma, mobs of white people massacred the Black community of Greenwood. Many among the mob were deputized by local officials and given firearms. Not only was it one of the worst incidents of racial violence in US history; it was also the first time US law enforcement dropped bombs on its own citizens. Tulsa is remarkable for the scale of the violence and the loss of resources that had been created in the Greenwood community, but the history shows there were about seventy instances of white terrorism upon large groups of Black people (Wilmington, Tulsa, Rosewood and Seneca Village, to name a few). Whether it's been the targeted murder of individuals or of whole communities, in the almost century and a half since Reconstruction ended, Black people have worked to build wealth and had their wealth destroyed over and over and over and over by external forces that kept resetting our community back to zero.

For over two hundred years the Monopoly game was being played on our bodies. We were not allowed to participate except as game pieces, building wealth for white people. And then we have almost ninety years—Jim Crow, post-Reconstruction— where, as we were building on our own, trying to pull ourselves up by our bootstraps, we were being brutalized. When we talk about the generational disenfranchisement that has limited the Black community's ability to grow its wealth, Reconstruction shows what we can do and who we have always been when we are not being suppressed at every turn. But slavery, Black Codes and Jim Crow are just some of what we've been up against from the beginning. If we go back to the Monopoly analogy, and you have a quarter of a century to build wealth by making sure the person that you're playing against can't make any money in the game, you can do pretty well. And if you can institute the Jim Crow system and claim the law is on your side as you brutalize and terrorize people for any development that threatens you, you can preserve your advantage. When so many white men who wore police badges during the day wore white hoods at night, they insured there would be no consequence for the lynching, theft and murders of Black people.

The extent of governmental complicity in the violence, impoverishment and theft endured by Black people, even after we were supposedly freed, is the foundation for our call for reparations. The government is responsible for fixing the wealth gap THEY CREATED. First by all the free labor that was extracted from generations of enslaved people as individuals and families built their wealth, but also as the US became a wealthy nation. On our backs. As we were repeatedly and systemically kept from building any wealth at all.

Even now, when Black people don't have to be concerned

about being robbed the way the Freedman's Bank robbed us, we are still getting robbed with mortgage rates. I have lived in high-end neighborhoods, middle-class neighborhoods, and the hood, and the difference is clear. Poor and lower-middle-class people have to pay higher rates on car loans, mortgages and personal loans, if they can get them at all. Insurers and banks have decided working-class neighborhoods are high-risk and have more crime, so the way to deal with people who are already economically disadvantaged is to disadvantage them more by making them pay more for everything. That's the answer of the white banking community. That's why I am a big advocate for Black banks. Why should you bank Black? Because it's time to stop the economic lynching.

We need to be taking advantage of Black banks' initiatives to make sure Black people are able to borrow for their homes and cars at lower interest rates. But also because if you're Black, the people working in the bank, and running the show, look like you. Wouldn't you like to bank where there isn't the implicit bias assuming you're a risky candidate? Wouldn't you rather start the conversation with an ally, rather than feel like you're about to be judged? Black banks are trying to be in the business of helping the Black community protect and grow its money. Even though the larger institutions a Black bank has to work with may limit what they can do, the goal is for them to be more flexible in how they work with community. The more of us that bank with Black banks, the more clout our banks will have. I would like to see us all banking at financial institutions like Citizens Trust in Atlanta or the Greenwood online bank or any other Black-owned, Black-run bank in your area.

The history is clear. The playing field has never been level, and as tired as we are of pushing uphill all the time, we have also lost patience with the white supremacist delusion that has persistently disenfranchised us on a national scale but wants to shrug and ignore all the ways they gave themselves a leg up while stepping on our heads. This late in the day, only action can be allowed to speak, which means that Black people need to get the same level of lending and community infrastructural support as has persistently been denied us during our four centuries in America.

When we talk about what has happened to us economically in America, we have to name all the brutalization we have experienced. And still, no matter how many times we have been knocked down, we've never stayed down. There has never been a single year in this country without systems in place to guarantee that we could NOT thrive. It's important to really let that sit with you awhile. AND YET, we have been driving and creating the culture of this country since we got here . . . with both of our hands tied behind our backs.

We have created Supreme Court justices, a president and vice president and countless successful entrepreneurs while being given no safe space to stand upon. We have spun magic out of thin air and raised children who have changed the country and even the world, and yet so many of us don't even know how we'll pay our rent or feed our families at the end of every month. Imagine who we could be if we had the same quality of education and opportunities as white people have always had.

THE GAME IS FIXED

Don't tell me white supremacy doesn't exist when the cops work as executioners for one population and PR managers for another.

—ALBERT LEE ON TWITTER (@ALBERTLEE2020)

Slavery is how we got here. Reconstruction was our brief moment in the sun. Jim Crow was America showing us how they really feel about us, and the Civil Rights Movement was the way we proved to ourselves that we could save our own lives. It's important that we don't lose sight of where we are on this journey. African Americans lived one experience of this country, and then the Civil Rights Movement detonated a bomb that shed a lot more light. It's one thing to say that we are our ancestors' wildest dreams. We are. Of course we are. But what happened when so many people laid down their lives for our equality in this country is that they changed the conversation and opened the way for us to know more and ask better questions than we ever had before. The Civil Rights Movement was powered by the clear vision that our equality was beyond dispute, and we were no longer willing to negotiate it with anyone. But in the midst of that clarity the game shifted, the rules changed and the system is still rigged.

So much of my activism and organizing has centered policing as the source of American injustice. When I read that the reason most white people can't imagine defunding the police is because they simply do not have negative encounters with police that lead them to believe the police are dangerous and uncontrolled, I actually despair for the future of this country. Policing and mass incarceration are probably the two places where the experiences of people of color are so divergent from white people that it is difficult to know what can be done to make white people open their eyes.

Like most Black people, I have horror stories from my experiences of the police. I have a traumatic story of being beaten up by the police. Here's one: when my son was six weeks old, I was pulled over by a white officer in Decatur, Georgia. He didn't like that I was asking him questions, and he put my baby's carrier in the street. Cars were swerving to keep from hitting my tiny baby. It would have only taken one driver, trying to see what the police were doing, not looking at the road, to accidentally kill my baby. This isn't the sort of thing a person does only once. That was the policeman's game. I can only imagine how many women he's done that to. It's deranged behavior, and someone that ill should not have a gun. And yet . . .

Now, my son is a six-foot-tall fifteen-year-old, and I worry about him constantly because he shares this world with police who see my sweet, well-mannered child as a pit bull. The real tragedy of what the police presence does to nonwhite people is it makes us afraid to be. I worry when my son is doing the most normal, ordinary things: hanging out with his friends, moving across the city on public transportation, anything. How does it serve either of us when I'm afraid to just let him be a kid? But this is part of where my sense of mission comes from. We have to change the culture so we can feel safe enough to just *be*.

History and the actual behavior of the police keep us from ever feeling safe in their presence. This survival sense that makes us recoil from the police makes the amount of time we spend protesting deaths at the hands of the police incongruous. We know who they are, we know what they do, and yet we are supposed to believe that after they've killed someone (as we could predict they would), justice is possible? Wouldn't justice be never having involved them in the first place?

What are we talking about when we say "justice" after a police killing? I want my son to thrive. I want to see him grow up. I want to meet the partner he will choose and see whether I get some grandkids out of the deal. When the police kill us, they are killing the dreams and the futures of the people who love them. Justice isn't money. Justice isn't a cop dying in jail for killing one of us. Justice is what is just and fair. What we deserve as humans living in the world is to live. I have protested with too many mothers who have lost their children to believe that any amount of money could ever make it right. When I am afraid for my son, just being in the world as a teenager, it's because I know what a mother's grief looks like. I have had enough negative encounters with the police to know they don't give a damn about me, or my friends, or my child. That is what is so scary about the police. They are humans who do not care about other humans. They are humans who lack empathy and feel it is appropriate to have power over other humans and the ability to treat them any kinda way they want. I'm not saying anything KRS-One wasn't saying in 1993, but where else can you see the behaviors and attitudes of slave masters and overseers than in modern-day policing? The hatred and disgust for the populations they deal with? The spitefulness? The willingness to kill anyone just because they can?

Most Black people, of any class, of any age, in any location, hesitate to call the police, even when they feel endangered. That speaks volumes. As we know from all the white people who call the police for everything from little girls selling water to birdwatchers, there is far more comfort for white people with the police. Having spent part of my childhood in a rural area before moving to Chicago, I had white neighbors who did far worse things while drunk than Rayshard Brooks did, and they did not lose their lives. I've seen non-Black family members get drunk and punch a cop, and of course, live to tell about it. If you're Black, you don't trust the police because your experience is that police assume you are a criminal even when you're doing nothing wrong. The police repeatedly deny their implicit bias, but the statistics and the news reports tell a very different story.

A while ago, a snippet from a 1975 documentary by Bill Moyers called *Rosedale: The Way It Is* went viral after it was rediscovered. The clip shows a group of Black kids on their bikes unknowingly ride into a white neighborhood where white kids throw rocks at them. Moyers interviewed the Black kids after, and we can see how surprised and hurt they were by the experience. This is worth talking about decades later because the white kids who threw those rocks are now CEOs. They are the police now. They are in Congress. If you are white, you may believe that open, naked racism is history, but 1975 was yesterday. It is still in the heart and under the surface, informing how some people interact with the world. What does implicit bias look like? Watch the *Rosedale* clip. That's one of its expressions.

The history of policing in the US is an ugly one. The first police forces in the country were created as slave patrols to surveil enslaved people as they moved through white spaces. Think on this for a moment. There were no police attending to crime on behalf of the general public, but there were organized groups of white men patrolling to make sure no slave could escape. Patrols had the right to punish any enslaved person that the patrol felt was not where they should be. This is important because it signaled to all white people—not just members of a patrol—that they had the power and the right to interfere with any Black person they encountered. Slave patrols existed until the end of slavery.

The loophole in the Thirteenth Amendment that allowed any Black person accused of a crime to be pressed into free service (slavery) was the South's way to continue to use slave labor. The goal was to incarcerate as many Black people as possible. The Black Codes created a system to incarcerate Black people for anything. If you were hanging out on a street corner, that was loitering, and you could get two or three years in prison for that. And once the Black Codes were in place, people were no longer incarcerated in a state-run facility; instead, they would be "loaned out" to plantations and other businesses that would have used slaves before emancipation. So you have the birth of policing and the birth of private prisons. Both systems are still in place, and sadly, they haven't changed much.

Policing starts with overseeing Black people, men especially, for the purpose of maintaining their enslavement. But here is where we have to pay attention to how slavery was justified. Slavery was justified by religion with the belief that Black people, in our nature, were not equal to white people and, having not been touched by a God they recognized, were no better than animals. Even in the North, and even among abolitionists during slavery, there was not a global belief that Black people were equal to white people. This matters because the South had the Thirteenth Amendment and its loophole creating opportunities for the re-enslavement of Black people, but in the North there is a disproportionate attention to Black people as though they cannot be trusted to abide by rules. The fact of slavery sets the tone across all American systems. The assumptions of white supremacy set the tone for all experiences of Blackness, regardless of geography.

By the time of the Great Migration, when unprecedented numbers of Black people moved from the South to the North, there is suddenly the same quality of racist law enforcement in the North as there had been in the South. Across the country, there is a very long history of police disproportionately paying negative attention to Black people and victimizing Black people regardless of their class, gender or age. When you hear people talk about the Green Book (*The Negro Motorist Green Book*) that Black people used from the 1930s to the 1960s as they drove across the United States, its purpose was to help Black people avoid the attention of police. It was a tool to enable them to go from one safe place to another safe place because sundown towns banned Black people after the sun went down, and simply being Black in the wrong place could get you killed. By the police.

So there has never been a moment when the police have been safe for Black people. Within this lack of safety, there is the financial motivation of mass incarceration that businesses benefit from, as they get free labor. The continued white supremacist delusion assigns criminality as the nature of Black people. This is the Black experience of law enforcement, generally. These are all historical truths, and I invite you all to research them, as the details reveal that the story is far worse than my brief summary.

Policing is the grandchild of slave catching, and the abuse and exploitation haven't stopped yet. But there is a moment in our recent history of policing that stands out as significant to how we arrived at this moment, with calls to defund the police and abolish the system of mass incarceration: the War on Drugs.

It's important to unpack the War on Drugs because it has impacts and implications in all Black communities across the country. In the 1980s, Ronald Reagan wanted to raise money to support the Contras against the Sandinista government in Nicaragua. This was effectively a civil war, and Reagan had no authority to meddle in the affairs of a foreign government. The Contras had the idea to run cocaine from Colombia to the US and use their profits to bankroll their war against the Nicaraguan government. The CIA was aware of it, and suddenly drugs were flooding into US cities. This marked the beginning of the crack epidemic.

Two things were happening simultaneously. In wealthy circles, cocaine was the fashionable drug. It was expensive and using it openly became a status symbol. In Black neighborhoods, crack, for which cocaine is the active ingredient, was much less expensive and very easy to find. And it's very addictive. Suddenly, the Black community was awash in a drug that is cheap and powerful, but because its effects don't last long, people quickly became addicted. Now, poor communities went from a poverty and desperation crisis to an addiction crisis. Parents were using and losing their kids. Young men caught selling crack got long jail terms because of mandatory minimum sentences. Possessing just five grams of crack (as either a user or seller) carries a five-year minimum prison sentence, but selling five hundred grams of cocaine (a more expensive product, with a richer, predominantly white clientele) earns the same five-year minimum sentence. Black people were penalized a hundred times more for using and selling the same drug. When you hear someone refer to the hundred-to-one sentencing disparity, this is what they're talking about. This is a story of unequal policing and racial profiling.

Reagan, who was continuing Nixon's War on Drugs, used the crack crisis to demonize Black men. Poor people and people of color were under siege in their communities, and one million Black men were imprisoned during this period, often for the possession of small amounts of drugs. Imagine the impact of taking one million people out of their communities, across the country. Many families lost fathers. Many families lost their primary wage earner. The scale of addiction and conviction in communities sent lots of children to foster care. This moment completely destroyed the fabric of Black families and devastated Black communities. This was racist policing of a problem created with the complicity of the government.

Clearly when Black communities do not trust police, it's a reflection of the malignant presence of police in Black communities and the history of racist, disproportionate enforcement. We didn't make that up. We didn't imagine it. This is verifiable history. It's worth recounting the history because when we are talking about poor communities in which Black people are being under-educated and there are no opportunities, it is not surprising when the best, brightest and the most entrepreneurial choose to sell drugs. It may be the only successful enterprise modeled in their environment. And that is a social problem. It isn't a criminality problem. It's a social problem and a poverty problem.

With the War on Drugs, mass incarceration exploded. But we know that it is difficult for felons to find work. A criminal record virtually guarantees, at best, a life of working at the minimum wage or returning to crime as the only way to support your family. Keith Strickland is a friend of mine who works with young men to educate them about the experience of incarceration in the hopes of keeping them committed to their education. He was arrested for the first time when he was only thirteen years old. Keith was already a convicted felon before he even knew what the word meant. What is the purpose of keeping young people in their prime out of the workforce? From the vantage point of communities of color, it just looks like a way to limit competition with the dominant culture.

If you are in a community that doesn't have many resources, you get a firsthand look at the ways policing can be opportunistic and predatory. I've been in neighborhoods where the police flood in on a Friday night and arrest as many people and write as many high-end tickets (no-insurance tickets) to people who are making $10 an hour. They know those folks are just trying to get through the day and feed their children. They need their car for transportation to work, but they can't really afford the car and the insurance. So the police find some people without insurance or without current registration. Maybe someone's license has expired. Yes, it's the law, but they are doing a sweep because the neighborhood is an easy target. They brutalize a bunch of poor people because they know they are economically disadvantaged and do not have the financial power to fight back.

Poverty creates crime. Period. The police go to these impoverished communities and brutalize the people every weekend by giving them $2,000 worth of tickets that they know the residents can't pay. Then they're put on probation until they work for free to pay it off. Or until they take every little extra dime that they have to pay it off. Or they get so frustrated because they're so traumatized by their experiences that they're incapable of coming up with the money, and one day the police catch them, and now they have a warrant, and they go to jail. And they sit in jail. And if they didn't have the money for that ticket, they damn sure don't have the money to bond themselves out. And now they're working as free labor again. And this is just one of many examples of how the police compound economic disadvantage. You can get a record for no reason other than being poor.

And here's the vicious cycle: now the neighborhood is considered to be a high-crime area. Banks don't lend in high-crime areas. Insurance on your car will be higher than in another neighborhood. The value of your house will be lower.

One of the ideas I would love to see become more mainstream, especially in our communities, is a bail fund. Some people lose years in jail because they can't afford to pay old tickets. They are being targeted simply because they are poor. But some of us have a little extra we can share, and I think this is a worthy way to help. It should be a human rights violation to criminalize poverty, but until that is acknowledged, and the laws are changed, let's spring our neighbors who are in jail for minor offenses.

In the struggle we often don't have enough time or the bandwidth to speak of our battle scars—the daily indignities of Black life. I'm thinking about all the Black men I've talked to who have been tased within an inch of their lives or the people in Bankhead harassed by police for tickets they can't pay.

A number of years ago, a couple of my friends who are authors invited me to a bookstore event in Athens, Georgia. Afterward I gave my friends Vania and Jessie a ride home. After dropping Vania off at her complex, I pulled out, and next thing I knew there were blue lights on me. I kept going until I could stop at a gas station. I didn't want to be pulled over in the dark.

I rolled the window down. Slowly. I said to Jessie, "Hand me my purse." The cop said, "Whoa! That's the kind of thing you people do that makes us nervous." I put my hands on the steering wheel and said, "You let me know when you're ready for me to get my license." After he did, he asked for my registration, and I said, "It's in the glove compartment. Do I have permission to take it out?"

He looked at it and went back to his car for a while. I said to Jessie, "Something ain't right; it shouldn't take that long. If they take me, tell them you will take my car." Then two more police officers drove up. One of the new officers walked up to my door and told me to get out. I complied, then he said, "You have a warrant."

As soon as he said it, I knew what it was: I had a bench warrant for unpaid tickets. A tropical storm had knocked the power out, so I didn't make it to my court date. I calmly explained why I hadn't paid, saying, "If you let me go, I can just pay the ticket now."

The officer said, "No."

Four more officers came, all of them with their guns drawn, and I started getting different commands. One said, "Put your hands on the car." One said, "Hands up." They all barked orders at the same time. "Can one person please just tell me what to do?" I pleaded. Were they going to shoot me?

One cop was irritated by me saying that, so he cuffed me and slammed me down face-first on the ground, and then one of them started punching me. All of this for an $85 bench warrant. They picked me up off the ground and put me in one of the police cars.

I started telling jokes, being silly, because someone had to deescalate this situation. The first officer came back to the car and ran Jessie's information through ICE. She's Latinx and was born and raised here, so nothing came up. They let Jessie take my car and she left to call my friend and writing partner, Gilly, who is also a lawyer. I sat in the precinct for thirty-six hours unprocessed, which meant no one could find me. I had to go to the desk to the sergeant and ask to be processed.

There was no women's holding cell, just a big room next to the desk with a row separating five females from fifty men. No one was really monitoring us. Periodically a guard would pass by and say, "Guys, don't talk to the girls, and girls, don't talk to the guys." There was always enough time between those announcements that anything could have transpired. Our only saving grace was we were in there with dudes who didn't want to do anything to hurt us.

The only thing I kept thinking was that it's Friday night and Sunday is my son's birthday. I'd had a whole set of events planned for him. My son loved Jason Reynolds and I was sched-uled to interview Jason in front of a live audience while playing a board game. For his birthday, my son was going to attend and get to hang out with his favorite author. I had convinced myself that if I got a transfer to my county, I could bond out. I could still make my son's birthday. I could still make my interview with Jason. I was the most annoying person in jail. I kept pressing the button every hour asking, "Where's my transfer? Process me." I was further humiliated when the person processing me was a woman whose kids I taught in summer camp.

Jail is not fit for humans. They gave us Kool-Aid packets that had to be mixed with water from the sink, and the sink water was recycled from the toilet. My face was cut up. I had a huge bruise on my jaw and cuts on my arms from when I hit the concrete. They gave me nothing for my face. I was on my menstrual cycle, and they gave me sanitary napkins one at a time.

There was a young woman who was eight or nine months pregnant. You are not allowed to lie down until lights-out, but pregnant women are allowed to. She asked for an additional mattress and the guards kept ignoring her. She was told that if she rang the bell again, she'd be in trouble. When she did, the response was to rough her up, cuff her and put her in solitary. Three Latinx women and one African woman were waiting on ICE transfers, crying and saying goodbye to their children over the phone. Jail is just a kennel. Kennels are probably nicer.

I finally got my transfer early morning on Sunday. And at that point I finally had to admit to myself that I was going to miss my son's twelfth birthday. I told my ex he should tell our boy that I was touring for the book and was detained. He might be upset with me, but at least he wouldn't have to worry about my safety or potentially feel ashamed that his mother had been arrested. My ex stopped me and said, "No, I'm gonna tell him the truth because there's no lie that will suffice." He said he wanted our child to know the extenuating circumstances that would cause his mommy to not be there. "And this would be a good time for me to talk to him about what we face."

It wasn't until Monday morning that I got to see a judge, then one of my brothers paid $85 and got me out. A weekend in jail and a waste of taxpayers' money spent for an $85 ticket. Later a Latinx friend who is white-presenting told me that her sister had the same kind of bench warrant and the police came to her house to arrest her. She offered to pay, they allowed her to get her checkbook and after that the officers left her in the safety of her home. All her story let me know is that there was a possibility the officer who stopped me could have done the same. He could see the warrant was for an unpaid ticket. There was another option available to him: to let me go—a moral option to let me go for something so minor, but that grace was not extended to me in the way it would have been extended to a white woman in that moment. The police too frequently believe that Black people have to be managed in a very aggressive way and there is an implied gentleness that has to be applied to all women except for Black women.

I was blessed at the time that my bosses at Little Shop of Stories were understanding. I was blessed that they were both people I could come to and tell this story to and explain why I missed work that weekend, and it was no problem. For some people, that would have cost them their job, and it would have had extreme financial consequences.

There's a scene involving a police stop that was supposed to appear in one of my books that I wasn't able to write: I had a full-blown panic attack and couldn't finish. Gilly, who was there, said to me, "I love you, but you have to get some help."

And I did. I found a therapist who could help me deal with my trauma and PTSD. The trauma we carry robs us in ways big and small.

The Monopoly analogy focuses on how owning land is the key to building wealth in the American capitalist system. The fact that Black people have not been allowed to own land in the same places, in the same ways, and with the same governmental support as white people explains why Black people do not have generational wealth. The absence of generational wealth in a capitalist system leads to poverty, so we cannot be surprised at the extent of poverty within the Black community. It is worth saying, however, that while Black people are politically scapegoated as the face of poverty (think of Ronald Reagan's "welfare queens"), there are more poor white people in America. There are more white people on welfare, using food stamps, whose children have free lunches in America. That's true because there are more white people in America. Period. So there's the poverty that's real, and there's the scapegoating about the poverty, which is a different thing entirely. In this condition of poverty, even people who own their homes don't have as much value assigned to their homes due to the history of redlining, and Black neighborhoods are less likely to have significant homeownership, so we can't be surprised when there is less investment in Black neighborhoods. This lack of investment results in phenomena like food deserts, which lead to poorer health outcomes and a lack of opportunity. And then, everyone is operating from a state of desperation and determined to make money however they can, but they are criminalized, despite the fact that the only way to make money is by criminal means. Which leads to a narrative of Black criminality that has never been true but has been prevalent in the American political conversation since slaves were trying to escape slavery.

There are particular moments that stand out in the criminalization of poverty. The War on Drugs is one. Another is the organization of the welfare system in the 1960s and 1970s, which broke up Black families because a mother would lose her family's benefits if there was a man living in the home. Policy makers, of course, failed to recognize that even if a man had been living in the home, his opportunities in his neighborhood were no better than the mother's. But all of this was an expression of the ways white people perceived Black behavior and sought to "correct or control" Black behavior.

Nothing about how we arrived in poverty is accidental. Nothing about how we arrived in poverty is surprising. What is surprising given the history is that any of us have managed to arrive in the middle class at all. But it is important to understand that to be Black and middle class is not the same as being white and middle class. In his book *Born a Crime*, Trevor Noah talks about the Black tax, which, as he explains it, is necessary because Black people have so few opportunities that when one of our number has an opportunity, she feels she must bring all of her people with her. A white investment banker who is enjoying a bonus of $2 million a year, every year, keeps that money. She invests her money and does whatever she wants with it. It's her money, and she has no obligations.

A Black investment banker, in the exact same situation, takes that bonus and buys one of her family members a house or helps her little cousins get cars. She uses that money for the benefit of her close family or her community. She feels obligated to do so. Not pressured to do so but obligated. She does it out of love but also because she recognizes that by being the exceptional one, she has an opportunity and understands that even the application of a little bit of what she has to the situations of the people she cares about would lift them up as well. But the fact that that's where her resources are going, that's the Black tax. She recognizes the luck of her experience and that if she doesn't create opportunities for other people, they will not enjoy that luck or any benefits that could push them forward. She reaches back and makes sure things work out for her people, but the Black tax means that she is more precarious and has less discretionary income than her white counterparts.

Take a moment to really reflect on that. Opportunity is so rare and so hard-won in the Black community that even a person who has worked her ass off to get to where she is recognizes that luck had as much to do with it as anything. We work hard in the hopes that if the stars align, and we just happen to be in the right place when the moon rises, we will have the chance to leverage our work into some tangible gain. And when we're lucky, we know that many, maybe hundreds, of our Black and Brown peers worked just as hard but won't have the same luck. So we try to be the agents of luck or goodwill for a few other people because we know, without a doubt, that it isn't their fault that the moon didn't happen to shine on them.

The reverse corollary to this is that there has never been an equation between wealth and value in the Black community. So few of us have had the opportunity to make any real money that, while it's an aspiration, it doesn't affect our self-definition. Many people tell stories about not being aware they were poor until they got older and had a reference point outside of their family or neighborhood. It is probably better for our mental health and self-esteem that we are not defined by the dominant culture's standards, but I would still like to see us get that loot.

Let's take that to the next step. The median Black household has one-tenth the wealth of the median white household. If you look at credit, if you look at the valuation of homes, a Black two-parent household, on average, has less wealth than a white single-parent household. In the Black community, the biggest correlation for wealth potential or high income is the education level of your parents, but how many Black parents even get college educations? We could talk about a rigged system, and that would be true, but the question is how to unrig the system. In talking about Monopoly, we've already mentioned the way opportunities were created. The solution has to be the end of redlining. The solution has to be the end of how credit potential is assigned to Black people, particularly those living in predominantly Black neighborhoods.

Let's make this relevant beyond the Black community. There's a McKinsey study of the wealth gap, and when it looks at how the quality of education corresponds to the neighborhood in which a school is located, there is an immense achievement gap between Black students and white students simply because Black students are being under-educated and their schools are under-resourced. McKinsey estimates that if there hadn't been an achievement gap, between 1998 and 2008, the US GDP would have been $525 billion higher. And if low-income students (not specific to race) had the same levels of educational achievement as richer students, the poorer students would have added $670 billion to the GDP by 2008. This matters. It doesn't just matter for Black people that we don't have the resources that allow us to thrive and prosper. It matters for the American economy. It is not just our crisis. It is an American crisis. It is what America is doing to itself, but it's hitting us hardest.

The economic precarity of the Black community also means that there is no guarantee that any one of us will be able to attain the same standard of living our parents achieved and that we were raised in. For white families, this would be an exception, not the rule. Think about what this means. You watch your parents scrimp and save and make wise choices, and they try to teach you how to manage money. You find that your situation doesn't allow you to save because you're servicing your student debt, and wages have not kept pace with the cost of living. We are constantly evolving and losing economic literacy. As a national community, we have watched as our middle class has grown, thanks to union jobs in the 1960s and 1970s, but with Reagan's privatization of services and union busting, the Black middle class has been shrinking ever since. The wealth gap is expanding because even though we can earn money, we have no foundation. Generational wealth is a foundation, and you build on top of it. If you have no foundation, you can keep throwing bricks on the ground, but that's not how you build a house.

There are some rich Black people, but imagine how big a Black tax they are paying. Our history is filled with folks who were rich once upon a time but died broke. It is still more difficult for us to create generational wealth than our white counterparts. That has to change.

I wish there were more research and more conversation about the mental health impacts of poverty. When you are poor in America, so much is done to shame you and to make you feel as though you have failed and in fact are a failure. You are made to feel that your definition as a person is as a failure. What I hope I have shown through the Monopoly analogy is that it never could have gone any other way. I'm not taking anything away from the exceptional Black people who have managed to leap forward to create different experiences in the present and for their future and the futures of their families. However, when we look at the precarity of Black wealth, as much as I give all the props to the exceptional folks who makes things happen, I never take it for granted that they, or their children, will occupy the same class position in a generation . . . in two generations . . . in five generations. I hope they will. But it is nothing we should take for granted.

When America, which has systemically and structurally denied our capacity to thrive at every turn, in every way, then turns around and shames any of us who need help but do not have resources—that, for me, is a crime. Then we are blaming the victim. But I want to discuss the mental health impacts of that poverty. I want to focus on the children who have had to live in fifteen different apartments by the time they're eighteen because their mother couldn't pay the rent due to circumstances that kept presenting, and they kept getting evicted. These children might have mental health issues. I want to talk about how those mothers, trying to keep the family together and trying to take care of their kids, are in a state of constant hypervigilance about all the things that could go wrong. Even when they are trying to rest, their minds are racing, making sure they have thought of everything they can do to keep things from breaking. They are hypervigilant when they're managing whatever has already gone wrong—laser-focused and more strategic than a general on the battlefield. That hypervigilance is an expression of trauma.

When people who need money have to engage with the systems that provide financial aid, whether it's welfare, food stamps or free health care, and they are treated like dirt, spoken to rudely and dismissed constantly. Their time is disrespected as they spend days waiting for services in offices with hundreds of other people. Every one of these events has a mental health impact. We have a system that negatively affects people's mental health, and those negative effects make it difficult for people to function. If we recognize that one in four people killed by the police had mental health issues, and we recognize that the system we live under has no interest in investing in mental health care, particularly for the poorest of us, then we are in the territory of human rights violations. We need to name the denial of basic human rights, and that begins with discussing the way the American system affects our mental health.

We also have to ask what quality of mental health care is out there for us when so few of the mental health professionals we encounter are likely to be culturally competent to understand our experiences. Only 5.3 percent of psychologists are Black. I want us to get rid of all the stigma we have against needing help and seeking help. But what is that worth if we can't find professionals who recognize our circumstances and our coping mechanisms and can help us without judgment grounded in their cultural context?

I'm focusing on poverty, but what does it mean to work in an office or to be an executive when you hear of another death of another Black person, and your white colleagues want you to make it okay for them? That's a mental health emergency. What does it mean to have to go to work in an office, or on Zoom, when you would rather be on the streets protesting with your people because this situation and the way Black lives are so disposable in America is breaking your heart and wrecking you emotionally? This is not just a mental health conversation about poverty. It's a mental health conversation about Blackness, and we haven't begun to address that because we don't have the resources or the professionals to address it.

HOW WE CAN WIN

I would love to see every company that profited from slavery pay reparations to the descendants of formerly enslaved people. This is already beginning to happen. The Jesuit order of the Catholic Church announced that it would be paying $100 million in reparations to the descendants of those who, for more than a century, were bought, sold and used by the Jesuits, who, in addition to using slave labor, engaged in the business of slave trading to raise money for the churches and schools they built, including Georgetown University in Washington, DC. This is a start, but it is clear that only when a shameful past of using slave labor or profiting from slavery comes to light do companies take steps to right their past wrongs.

Now is the time to present our receipts and imagine our way forward. In fact, this is an exciting time because so many great minds are thinking on these questions from so many different angles. For this fight, this stand for equity in a country that owes us everything, we have fifty years of our own

PhDs and specialists who have detailed our history, done the accounting on what (in real money terms) this country has cost us and how much it has made on our backs—pimping our labor, stealing our resources and cultural capital, killing us. Today, we're not making this case based only on our (correct) feelings. We have mountains of data to back it up. Our receipts are objective facts. When I'm telling our history or imagining how we can win, I'm leaning on the work of my sisters and brothers who are doing the work that moves us forward. I'm here for all of it. I love the way these questions—how do we address the history to make America accountable for its treatment of us? And how do we get the answers to those questions in the form of equity?—have become showcases for so much Black talent and excellence in economics and the social sciences. Bring it, y'all! The Black brain trust lifts us all up.

My vision of how we can win focuses on a few details in our recent history and current situation as a way to talk about the systems that have disenfranchised us and the fixes necessary for us to actually thrive in this country. It's not everything. The list could be one hundred times longer, but it's a few broad strokes to paint the picture. When we, as Black people, feel that great harms have been done to us, we're not wrong, but we keep being told that we're whining and that we're living in the past. The point of this history is to show that the past we're living in is the one we were brought here for and have never been allowed to exit. No group of people are more forward-looking than African Americans, who have been driving the culture in this country since we arrived. But are we still living in the pain, dysfunction and harm of the past? Damn straight we are. And we won't get out of here until we name what that looks like and feels like. We're going to have to heal ourselves. That's our job. But we also have to hold this country accountable for repairing all the damage done. America is only America because of what it could become by standing on our backs. This country owes us everything. We should never be shamed or embarrassed to name that truth.

For too long, we have been having a conversation about us on someone else's terms. We need to stop being willing to respond to people who think we should be pulling ourselves up by our bootstraps or who believe the specious claim that we're lazy or naturally criminal-minded, wielded by people who feel entitled to our labor, our ideas and our culture. We might have to explain to other people of color who talk about how they came to America and were able to prosper. They may not understand why Black people haven't done as well because they are leaning into their proximity to whiteness. A certain unnamed former president created an awakening for people of many minority groups with his explicit racism, but for those who still haven't caught up, it's worth saying that we were positioned at a disadvantage so long before their ancestors touched American soil that we are trying to address wrongs done before they started paying attention. Or maybe, instead of explaining anything, we need to speak about the entitlement we've earned with blood to every single thing this country has.

We know that the game is rigged. The question is, how can it be changed to make it fair? We've taken our four hundred turns of playing as well as we could while others cheated, changed the rules, cheated some more and broke up the place when they got bored of just cheating. We have already demonstrated that when they're playing Monopoly and we're playing survival, we can't ever win. Now it's time to ask different questions. Now the question is, what would winning look like? And how do we get there? We can't go back in time; we can only move ahead. But before we do so we need to change the game. We need to change the board. We need Reconstruction 2.0.

RECONSTRUCTION 2.0

What is it you want me to reconcile myself to? I was born here almost sixty years ago. I'm not going to live another sixty years. You always told me it takes time. It's taken my father's time, my mother's time, my uncle's time. My brothers' and my sisters' time, my nieces' and my nephews' time. How much time do you want for your progress?

—JAMES BALDWIN, FROM A 1984 INTERVIEW INCLUDED
IN THE DOCUMENTARY *The Price of the Ticket*

The R-word used to be a fantasy. We knew we deserved reparations after all Black people have experienced in this country, but we couldn't imagine how such a thing might actually happen. The fact that we are now talking about reparations, prison abolition, defunding the police and more is an expression of a greater number of Black folks with access to power, and greater outrage at the treatment of Black people by systems, such as policing. I want to take this conversation one step further. Equity across all of America's systems. Every. Single. One. I want to see reparations fund a ground-up overhaul of what this country is and how it operates. I think we're overdue for Reconstruction 2.0.

In order to have a real conversation about reparations and what Reconstruction 2.0 would involve, we have to name a handful of things that for me are not controversial. The Brookings Institution says:

> In 1860, over $3 billion was the value assigned to the physical bodies of enslaved Black Americans to be used as free labor and production. This was more money than was invested in factories and railroads combined. In 1861, the value placed on cotton produced by enslaved Blacks was $250 million. Slavery enriched white slave owners and their descendants, and it fueled the country's economy while suppressing wealth building for the enslaved. The United States has yet to compensate descendants of enslaved Black Americans for their labor.

We need to make distinctions between opportunity costs—the costs to us of opportunities we never had because of the systems and racism we have lived under for four hundred years. The opportunities we never had includes lives lost, generational wealth that was never amassed, all the innovations and creative contributions never made. When we talk about every business that was burned down, every patriarch that was lynched. If we were to use Tulsa and its Black Wall Street as an example, there were thriving businesses and thriving families. Everyone who wasn't killed in the massacre lost everything. Even if they were poor by the standards of Black Wall Street, they were likely doing better than other Black folks in the rest of the country. If you were to think of the children of the families of Black Wall Street, what are the odds any of them went on to college, even though that would have been an assumption for their lives before the massacre? After the massacre, they no longer had resources or community support. Everything that was lost closed doors on opportunities that should have been.

We could tell the story of lost opportunity all day long, every day. Everyone who has ever gone to substandard schools to be contained rather than educated is a lost opportunity. If we were to assume that even half of them are actually geniuses or that they could have gone on to professional employment and because they were under-educated never had that opportunity, then again we're talking about lost opportunity. So the problem we have, really, is limiting the number of metrics we want to bring into the conversation about what needs to be considered for us to arrive at equity. Effectively, we have lived in a 120 percent onslaught for four hundred years. Every aspect of life could be the detail we use to talk about where compensation needs to be assigned in the idea of reconstruction. That is how bad and desperate the situation has always been. Even now the situation is that bad and desperate. Particularly when you think of every person who never had the opportunity to go to college simply because of finances, simply because of how poor their elementary through high school education was. When you think of everyone who, for lack of opportunity, took their entrepreneurship to the streets and sold an illegal substance, all of these are the expressions of lack of opportunity, lack of resources, lack of possibility. And all of that is a demonstration of lack of equity. The conversation could be virtually infinite. But these are some of the things that I'm paying attention to—and I do not think this is an exhaustive list—and I invite everybody to think about how we should have this conversation and add to this conversation.

The truth is this: if reparations were to be paid, they would far more likely be paid in the form of institutional resources rather than checks of $200,000 or a half million or whatever amount could be decided upon. That's not a bad idea because, on the one hand, structural issues are what brought us here, and so structural changes should walk us out of here. But on the other hand, I would also say if handing out reparations checks replicated what social scientists have seen happen to lottery winners, that would be tragic. For most big lottery winners, they get their big windfall, buy everything they wanted and go everywhere they imagined; then a few years later, they have the same amount or less than they had before they won the lottery. This is a phenomenon that crosses race and class. It would hurt my heart to see the hood filled with Bentleys one year, but two years later, we're watching them all get repo'd, and people don't have enough money to feed their kids. Social scientists think this happens as an expression of the way we think about money. People who don't have the experience of managing big money don't tend to know how to manage a lot of it when they suddenly have it. You know I'm all about the economics of our situation. I want to see my people thrive and prosper in deep and real and enduring ways. I want us to finally have the opportunity to build generational wealth, so I would like systems to change rather than checks to be cut for individuals.

First and foremost, this is a strategic plan for us. White America has had four hundred years to train us to a view of scarcity. We have been traumatized at so many levels that even those of us who were raised in wealth and comfort often fear that it can all be taken away in a minute. That's what trauma does. It makes you live in two worlds at the same time. The world your body is inhabiting may be comfortable, but your spirit doesn't believe any of it and is making plans to serve whatever trauma has taught it. So we believe in scarcity. We believe that there will never be enough for us. We believe we will never have all we really want, and when we get fierce and formidable, we expect to be killed or dismissed. We don't trust this world. And that's training. That's what America has taught us. We consume like crazy because we want to grab at least a little bit of something while we can.

One of the places where community economics intersects with our trauma is the way we do not trust money we can't see. We are in a negative feedback loop. So many Black people have lost everything, so many times, we want the physical object of money rather than the idea of money. Looking at a spreadsheet that details your wealth (home, investments, money market accounts) is the idea of money. The money is real, and it's really ours, but we would rather have cash money hidden in our homes or on our bodies where we can see it and touch it. So we have created a culture that values name brands and bling, objects we can wear, and for many of us, if we don't have those objects, we feel poor and less than. That's what makes someone step through a broken glass window. . . . The dream is stacks of Gs in our hand. This is especially true for Black men, who feel like, living with a target on their backs, they want to wear all their wealth as armor. It isn't true that being iced up intimidates a cop who has decided today is not your day. But in America, where capitalism is king, it feels like it should be true.

And yet, this generational wealth I want for all my people is created by owning property. You don't own it until it's all paid off and the deed is in your name. And when that happens, the value of your property is that you can use it, and you can borrow against it if you have to. It isn't as sexy as designer clothes, but it is the cornerstone to building wealth. Cash money in your hand is an invitation to spend. Wealth is about saving and investing.

WHAT THE GOVERNMENT CAN DO FOR US

It is important that this not be allowed to become a conversation about worthiness. How did we earn this? More than two centuries of slavery and everything that came after. Enough said. We are owed. We're here to collect. We must have a plan that is created specifically for African Americans, because as a nation we are going to have to be intentional as we fix the generational, economic and social apartheid that has crippled Black growth in America.

One of the things this country needs in order to get to equity through a peaceful process is something like a truth and reconciliation commission. Many people feel that when South Africa, at the end of apartheid, went through truth and reconciliation, it required a lot of forgiveness on the part of people who had been harmed. And maybe not enough change on the part of the people who had done the harming. Still, it was largely successful in South Africa, and it's worth considering. As a restorative justice practice, truth and reconciliation invite conversations that have not been had in this country. That's vitally important, but even more important is the language the process would introduce. We do not have enough common language to talk about difference and the experience of exclusion. We have not looked at the stereotypes and systems and unpacked them in the context of history and who benefits from their continued use. The dominant culture has not had to acknowledge the embedded harms in the systems they created because they are not listening to those communications so that solutions that are agreed to will actually be instituted and enforced. Truth and reconciliation would be a confrontation with history that is long overdue.

At the tail end of the Civil War, multiple things happened that directly harmed Black people. Newly freed people were promised forty acres and a mule, began to receive land and then had it taken away and were attacked violently. President Andrew Johnson used our situation as a tool to position himself in relationship to Southern former landowners, which came at the expense of Black people. We were a political casualty because the Democrats—the Southern secessionist party, at that time— recognized that with emancipation, formerly enslaved people who had been counted as three-fifths of a person (as the result of the Three-Fifths Compromise) and had not been allowed to vote would now be counted as whole people. If they were allowed to vote, they would vote Republican, the party of Lincoln, and the Democrats would have no path to future political victory. All of these factors contributed to creating a system, the harms of which we are still feeling the effects. And more layers of harm were added to that over time.

If we were to have a truth and reconciliation commission, it would require unpacking this history and presenting the receipts of the harms that have been done. The government (and maybe some corporations) would have to address those harms and set them right. That seems like a very worthy process because the path to equity is in naming and untangling each harm and assigning numerical money values to the cost of those harms. What I particularly appreciate about the idea of a truth and reconciliation commission is that the real point of it is that people become accountable for the harms. White America has a way to say, "Well, it might have been my grandfather who benefited from the harm, or my great-grandfather who perpetrated the harm, but I never had a slave and none of this has anything to do with me." The truth and reconciliation process would locate white privilege in its very distinct economic evolution that begins in slavery. It's critical to negotiating our way to equity. It's hard for me to imagine how we will arrive there with all parties accountable and in a state of recognition of harms without such a public, detailed airing of how we got here.

When we talk about Reconstruction 2.0, it's imperative that we move in two directions at the same time. It won't be enough to create new systems intended for greater equity. We also have to think deeply about dismantling old, entrenched systems that have marginalized us, impoverished us and kept us out of equal participation in the American economy. We have been denied opportunities to develop skills and tools that other people have. Generational wealth is a tool. It's a foundational tool for building more wealth, and we haven't had access to that tool. Education is also a tool, and the property tax funding of education with the marginalization and localization of Black people in neighborhoods that are disadvantaged has meant we have not had, generally, access to the tool of good education. Reconstruction 2.0 needs both approaches. One approach will not work. Too much has been done. Too much water is already under the bridge. What we need is investment in every aspect of the lives of Black people and Black communities. If we're honest, even if the government undoes all of what has been done to hold us back and creates the conditions for us to have all the tools we should have had all along, we will still need generations to reach financial and economic parity with the white community. Our situation is that deep and that devastating.

The very first thing I want is the reinstitution of the Freedmen's Bureau. And if we don't call it that, there needs to be an agency that's allowed to complete the work the Freedmen's Bureau was meant to do in the first place, which is to create economic advancement for African American people in order to balance out the fifty-yard head start that white people were given in terms of building wealth and a strong economic base for their communities. It's time to allow it to complete the job it began. It was a good idea and it showed great promise, but it was never allowed to complete its mission. In truth, it was barely allowed to begin. The impulse for the Freedmen's Bureau was the recognition that after generations of being impoverished, people needed, at minimum, enough tools and resources they could use to create a life on their own terms. Formerly enslaved people needed safety and protection and an even playing field. We still need those things. There is some precedent for this. Reparations were paid to Japanese Americans after they were interned during World War II.

In my imagination of the new Freedmen's Bureau, there would be a department for everything: for education; for economics; for medical care (which would include therapy and drug counseling). The War on Drugs broke up so many families and sent so many children to foster care that between healthy family systems that were broken by slavery to the devastation of families in the 1980s and 1990s, I think family therapy should be mandated as well.

There is a lot that the Freedmen's Bureau should make itself responsible for. First and foremost, my top two on my Freedmen's Bureau 2.0 list are: (1) end education funding based on the local tax base. When I think about this, the only way that this will really work is if we had national standards of education. The reason is that *Plessy v. Ferguson* created the legal idea of "separate but equal," and we know how unequal we were treated in our separation. The Constitution allows the idea of states' rights. Part of what that has meant is states that value education put money into it. States that do not, do not. Poor states do not privilege education, and poor people in poor states get it worst of all. What we are talking about is guaranteeing quality education, and the only way to do that would be through national standards. We need national standards for education because, right now, standards higher than local public schools often exist in the form of charter schools, which, when created in underprivileged, minority neighborhoods, invite gentrification. Soon gentrifiers are bringing a different set of values and changing the whole school.

(An aside: I wish gentrifiers cared about how unwelcome they are. Nothing is a better example of the white supremacist delusion than white people who arrive in a neighborhood only to try to remake it in their own image. The delusion believes itself to be the standard for all things. It isn't interested, isn't even curious, about what it doesn't know and what isn't like it. We have had to pretend to be like them in order to function in workplaces, not because what and who we are can't do the job just as well, but because those who are in the delusion can only see themselves reflected. They can't see us as ourselves, only as *not them*. When we are not serving their image of what value is, we have no value. It's unbearably tiresome. This madness has to stop.)

I would love to see quality education guaranteed by a national curriculum taught in every public school, to every student, K–12, across the nation, because it would end this problem. It would guarantee that whether you were in a rich neighborhood or an abjectly poor one, your child would be getting the same education, at the same level and of the same quality. This is one of the minimum standards. Without guaranteeing every child of color a quality education, you can't guarantee anything else. That's basic.

The second item on my list would be abolition of the carceral state. Is that the same as saying defund the police? Hell yes, it's the same thing. We went from slave catchers to a loophole in the Thirteenth Amendment that allowed Black people to be pressed into free service (slavery under a different name) if they were convicted of a crime and the militias that made sure enough people were convicted to keep plantations humming with free labor. Modern-day policing (and its priorities) evolved from this legacy.

DEFUND THE POLICE AND ABOLISH CARCERAL SYSTEMS

It's important that we come to terms with the ways we've been treated. We have been held to a social contract while few of its benefits have ever been extended to us. The respectability politics of Black people policing each other so we don't scare white people has been our big move to show that we're worthy of being included in the social contract. But has it worked? Black people are still being killed for no reason other than their skin. Defunding the police is a crucial step in ending the pretense that what policing is doesn't, by its nature, exist to criminalize us and to exclude us from a position of equity and equality in the social contract.

There has been a lot of propaganda to make people feel as if by advocating for defunding the police we are trying to have a negative effect on public safety. That is not what is being said. The Defund the Police movement is saying we need to reallocate funds so that we are more productively utilizing the police department. It takes you longer to get a barber's license and a cosmetology license than it does to become a police officer. The training is not extensive enough. We are not doing the proper mental health checks to make sure police are healthy enough to interact with the public. In cities, we are over-policing marginalized neighborhoods in order to make budgets.

In other countries in the global North, imprisonment does not involve punishment but rehabilitation and retraining. Prison systems with the lowest rates of recidivism (people returning to prison after being released) treat criminal behavior as a developmental or social anomaly and work with their population to create other options. We do not do that. We only punish, and the nature of punishment is that anyone who arrives in the prison system, even as a low-grade offender, is hardened into a criminal in the course of their incarceration. We make people unfit to live in society, and when they're released, we have a society with an increasing number of unfit people. This isn't a winning strategy, and it doesn't make sense that this is our chosen approach. But it is what we do. Other countries apply different approaches with far better outcomes. We don't lack models for better ideas. And let me say this: as marijuana is decriminalized and legalized in the US, every nonviolent person who has been locked up for dealing or possession should be released and their records should be expunged. This would be one way to begin to address some of the wrongs inflicted by the War on Drugs. It would be another kind of injustice for corporate structures to make bank off cannabis while people continue to languish in prisons.

Defunding the police remains a controversial idea for some people, but the idea of defunding is grounded in the fact that the cost of policing and mass incarceration is not actually justified by the results. It is estimated that the United States spends more than $100 billion a year on policing and more than $182 billion a year on incarceration. From the perspective of the defunding movement, this $282 billion a year is not actually increasing safety by any measure. But people, especially people of color, are endangered and dying for no good reason. More to the point, the police are used as the antidote to many problems for which the police are not trained to handle. Police respond to mental health calls. Police respond to family disputes. Police respond to child truancy. Police respond to any number of circumstances for which law enforcement is not the place where the solution will be found because the problem is not an expression of criminality. It is a social problem.

There's an expression: if all you have is a hammer, everything looks like a nail. The police have one form of training that involves shooting and subduing. Recent cases have revealed that the police seem to not even distinguish bystanders or children in a response situation. Their mode is to assert authority, threaten or do violence. We all know what they do, so when cops show up, we know what to expect from them. By continuing these practices, police are becoming one-trick ponies who have one skill set, and I would go as far as saying that some people who choose to become police officers have drunk the Hollywood elixir and imagine themselves as badasses, bursting through doors, talking tough, beating somebody down. They want to be action heroes. That is not what we need. We don't need action heroes. We need people who have a grounding in our communities and who are invested in the health and safety of our people. We need people who believe that their job is to move through a space fixing problems and helping people, and that is very, very different than the way police tend to see themselves or understand their job. So the point of defunding the police is to recognize that most of them are hammers, but most situations are not nails.

Dr. Cedric Alexander, author of *The New Guardians: Policing in America's Communities For the 21st Century*, is a former Deputy Chief Operating Officer for Public Safety in DeKalb County, Georgia, who also served on President Obama's task force on twenty-first-century policing. When he joined the force in the 1970s, the focus of law enforcement was public safety, and he argues that the cop-as-warrior model needs to shift back to officer-as-guardian.

The police have just become the military against the people. Look at their uniforms. Look at their training. A lot of equipment they have they don't need: no police department needs a tank. If there's some tank-level shit, call the National Guard. That's what the National Guard is for.

Caring for the public should be more about solid public safety. I don't want the dangerous few to be able to harm us, and public safety involves safeguarding people from crime, disaster and other potential threats. When most people think about public safety, though, they think of the police, but really that also involves others like firefighters, EMTs, parole officers. All of these people have to work together better to offer correction and incorporate mental health. And then all of these departments need some kind of coordinated training to grapple with how they intersect with each other in order to truly protect the people. We need the guardians of the community we deserve.

By dealing with problems in their expression phase rather than at the root, we are neglecting to find solutions. If our focus was on the number of people with untreated mental illness, we would devise a strategy to give better care to mentally ill people. Instead, as I've said before, one in every four people killed by the police was mentally ill. That's inhumane. And it's inhumane to apply brute force to any nonviolent social problem. If 80 percent of arrests nationwide are for minor offenses rather than serious crimes, we would do better to attend to why those minor offenses occur. How many Black people have been pepper-sprayed or killed in traffic stops? Maybe there should be a better way to make sure car registration is current or a broken taillight gets fixed. It's clear the police cannot be trusted to do something so simple.

And really, at the heart of this issue is the unequal use of force. It matters that policing has slave catching as its foundational DNA. White people are not killed by police in casual traffic stops because they are not assumed to be violent or dangerous, even when they are. There is no amount of too calm, too polite or too communicative for a Black person in an engagement with the police. Any one of us could be killed for no reason. A system that actively disavows its own stated assumption that everyone is innocent until proven guilty is a rotten system. In neighborhoods of color, people often do not report being the victim of a crime because of the high likelihood of their being further victimized by the responding police. Couple that with the fact that there is little evidence that a police presence deters crime, and we have a high price tag for an unaccountable system that destroys the social fabric. How can anyone defend this as a good idea? If we took half of the national policing and incarceration budgets and spent that money on creating equitable education with a unified national curriculum, every child would have a chance to succeed. Dead-end lives without opportunity would be relegated to the horrors of the American past.

Defunding the police is the best idea if this country is finally ready to recognize the ways policing is completely incongruent with its stated values. In the meantime, while we are having this conversation at the level of city councils and states, we must, at least, end qualified immunity. Qualified immunity is the legal protection that makes it especially difficult to prosecute murderous police. That unaccountability allows them to feel protected and invincible as they're shooting someone in the back or kneeling on a man's neck. The end of qualified immunity is the absolute minimum legal step to protect our lives and have a means to prosecute police.

The $182 billion a year we spend on mass incarceration would be better spent on rehabilitation, retraining and transformative justice. It is also worth recognizing that people of color are incarcerated at a far higher rate for much smaller crimes. The courts are beginning to recognize that locking people up for long sentences in the prime of their lives over small offenses is both unduly expensive for the state and creates the condition of more desperation (and possibly crime) in the long term. Prison abolition is an important conversation that invites us all to think in new ways about the social contract, what we owe each other and how we can approach nonsocial behavior in ways that weave a person back into society rather than abandon them. It's a healing approach, and this country needs some new ideas for healing above all.

OUR NEIGHBORHOODS

In the realm of real estate, there needs to be investment in Black communities. This is a tricky one because as we have seen, no sooner does investment come into Black communities than white people who consider themselves "urban pioneers" come in droves to gentrify the area and displace Black people. The question becomes: Is there a way to protect historically Black neighborhoods and cap the percentage of non-Black or non–people of color residents allowed to own property in such a community? I don't see any other way to protect Black communities. We need the investment, and we need the protection.

When we advocate for that protection, it's very important to acknowledge that historically Black communities are a repository of Black *cultural* wealth. You cannot have the gentrification of Harlem without losing a lot of African American cultural knowledge. We have to be mindful of protecting our heritage as we move forward. (An aside: I would make the distinction that when white people talk about heritage, they are inevitably trying to protect monuments paying homage to seditionists and Confederate flags. When Black people talk about protecting our heritage, we're talking about protecting spaces in which Black excellence was born and has thrived. Our heritage is a positive story, not a negative denialist story.) Even though redlining officially ended with the Fair Housing Act of 1968, in practical terms it has never ended. By 1968, neighborhoods that were historically Black were already significantly poorer than a similar white neighborhood nearby. Because the neighborhoods were poorer and insurance was more expensive, but housing valuations were lower and no work was done to respond to that history, Black neighborhoods remained undervalued. This is what has made them targets for gentrification.

Redlining has officially ended, but now all the effects of redlining have to be fixed. Insurance prices and mortgage rates have to be reset. Home prices need to be reset in Black communities—not to price Black people out but to add value to Black homeownership. The point is to finally invest in Black people and Black homeownership in the same ways white people benefited when the US government was intent on growing its middle class. It's time for the government to invest in Black wealth creation.

There needs to be a legal path for redress for Black families that have unfairly had their homes or farms or land taken away. This has happened in so many ways. Predatory lending is one of the most common, and there needs to be a legal way to cure those harms. When Black people have borrowed money at predatory rates because that was all that was available to them and the result of those predatory rates has meant they could not sustain the terms, we have to acknowledge that the roots of our vulnerability to predatory practices are the structural ways we've been shut out of homeownership.

With the end of redlining, we also need to give favorable rates for business loans in the Black community. I don't actually want to limit this to the Black community. Black people are charged more when we borrow money. The reason we pay higher rates is grounded in all the structural inequities that Reconstruction 2.0 must address. One of the effects of this inequity is Black entrepreneurs often start their companies by taking money out of their 401(k)s or using their savings. In order to build something, for lack of other options, they have to risk everything. Black entrepreneurs have less of a financial cushion when they begin, which makes them more likely to fail. And depending on the type of business, a Black business owner may be less likely to open in a Black neighborhood, simply because fewer people have money to spend on nonessential services. The effect is that community reinvestment for us, by us, ends up being shallower than it would be in a white community. If we had investment zones that created opportunities for entrepreneurship in the Black community and if loans were given that were reasonable and accessible to Black entrepreneurs, we could change the face of our communities.

RAISE THE MINIMUM WAGE

We have to raise the minimum wage. In the Black community, where chronic under-education has been a feature of our experience, we have consigned people to live and work at the minimum wage for the length of their lives. In response to calls to raise the minimum wage, some politicians say that the minimum wage was not created for people to live on or to raise families on. In their minds, it was created as a first step for people who need to gain work experience (for example, teenagers with their first jobs). That has not been the circumstance for poor people, and being stuck at the minimum wage has particularly been an issue for Black and Brown people and immigrants.

If you want young Black men to stop selling drugs, then you have to give them a real opportunity. When young Black men cannot begin their lives because they have not been educated;

because they live in areas that don't have any opportunity; because the minimum wage is so low, they can't buy a car and put gas in it; they can't have a car and pay insurance on it; they can't re-register their car after saving for two years to buy a car and get it set up. When that is the circumstance, and all that's available is minimum-wage jobs, how rational would it be to say this is the limit of my possibility? How would taking two or three jobs at the minimum wage to support myself and my family be a rational choice in a world where there are other possibilities to work less and make more? Economists are invested in the idea of consumers as rational actors, but when a poor person makes a rational choice to do something illegal because that is the best option in his environment, he's criminalized and disproportionately prosecuted. I may have issues with the effects of drugs on the Black community, but it's no mystery why some people feel selling is the best choice they can make.

CIVIL RIGHTS

In the realm of civil rights, we need the government to commit to Black equity. The minimum requirements for equity in this landscape would be fixing the Thirteenth Amendment and making ironclad civil rights and voting protections. We have to begin there. We also need the US to enshrine education as a right. The United Nations declared education as a right in 1948, and yet, more than seven decades later, we still do not guarantee every child a quality education.

It is clear that America is committed to gun ownership. And it's equally clear that there is a seemingly infinite number of unstable white men who want to kill people and white supremacists who believe a gun is their best tool for maintaining the status quo. We need to clearly define what a hate crime is, and we need to support other communities of color in that conversation. In my definition of a hate crime, police who kill us because of racist assumptions are committing a hate crime. But the definition needs to be far more rigorous than that. We have to end qualified immunity for police. I know I included that in the conversation about defunding the police, but qualified immunity allows police to get away with violating our civil rights, so while it's a talking point in the reasons to defund the police, it is also a civil rights issue.

DOCTORS AND TEACHERS

Black people (in general) have a well-founded distrust of the medical establishment. James Marion Sims, considered the father of modern gynecology, did harrowing experiments on enslaved women. The Tuskegee syphilis experiment led a group of men with syphilis to believe they were being treated while doctors actually did nothing. They recorded the progression of the illness as the men went blind and fell into mental illness. The study would have continued, presumably until every member of the 400-person cohort died, if the details had not been leaked to the press in 1972. By that point, the study had already been underway for forty years. In that time, 128 participants died, though the observing doctors had the means to cure them. Cancer cells cultured from the body of Henrietta Lacks were taken without her consent and have become one of the most important cell lines in medical research. Her cells changed the medical world, and she still has family members who are on public assistance. Though her cells generate millions each year for the pharmaceutical companies that use them for research, her descendants have never been compensated. The medical establishment has a lot to live down. That's not even half of the history worth telling, but it's a taste.

If you're Black, it's rare not to know a medical horror story, either your own or that of someone close to you. During my pregnancy, I had a white ob-gyn, and during one of the prenatal checkups, the doctor casually says, "You have a weak cervix, so the baby will be premature." No bedside manner. And I can't imagine he would have spoken to a white woman the same way. My mind was racing with concern for my child, but it was clear he didn't really care. I was already nervous because Black women die in childbirth in much larger numbers (two to three times more often) than white women because when Black women are telling doctors that something is wrong, they have to overcome the preconceived notion that we are intellectually inferior, that we couldn't possibly know our bodies well enough to sense something wrong, and we're ignored. I had to get to some Black doctors, who explained what they could do to make sure my baby arrived safe and sound. In my hunt for a second opinion I found Dr. John R. Lue, who was an obstetrician-gynecologist here in Atlanta but is now in Augusta, Georgia, and is affiliated with Augusta University Medical Center. He examined with gentleness, something not often exercised toward Black women, and then said to me, "Don't worry, we're going to get this baby here safely." He then referred me to a specialist, one of his fellow Morehouse alumni, who I'd need to see simultaneously. My son is fine, but even now, more than a decade later, I really do believe if I hadn't left that doctor's office and made sure I was surrounded by Black doctors for the rest of my pregnancy, the whole story would have been different.

It's important that we recognize that one of the most pernicious effects of having no generational wealth is that without that wealth, we have not managed (and how could we?) to create the resources we need within our community. Medical school, law school, postgraduate education: these are expensive. If you have little or no generational wealth, you're going to have to take out all the loans in order to attend higher education. What this means is that when you're finished with law school, medical school, engineering, etc., you're going to *have to* take a big corporate job that guarantees you can afford to survive while you're paying back all the money you borrowed. How does that affect the Black community? Very simply, it means that we bleed our smartest and our best into corporate structures—whether it's corporate health care, corporate law or banking—simply because they have to pay their student loans. So when we need representation, those lawyers are quite often not in our communities. When we need Black doctors—therapists, oncologists, ob-gyns, pediatricians—they are not in our community because they cannot afford to serve the communities they came from.

This is a matter of life and death for us. Just like staying with the white doctor while I was pregnant felt like it could have been the death of my child. In 2016, a group of medical students were polled about different myths the medical establishment has long believed about Black people. Every one of those myths has been debunked and every one of them, if they were believed, would affect the quality of care given to a Black patient. Most of the white medical students thought at least one of the myths was true. Depending on the doctor and the myth they believe, that might result in shabby, uninformed care, or care that is overly painful or dangerous. In the twenty-first century. It's inexcusable that this is the way science affects us, in one of the most technologically advanced countries in the world. The gift of being alive at this time is that there are lots of studies that give us real-world metrics about the cost of not having the care of doctors that look like us. The best outcomes in health for Black people are with Black doctors. That's true for your newborn in the neonatal unit, and it's true when you're giving birth. It's true across the board. It is already a problem that we don't have doctors proportionate to our population (roughly 6 percent of doctors and surgeons are Black, but we are 14 percent of the population), but we may not even have access to the doctors that exist. And we need them focused on problem-solving in our community.

All of this goes back to money. Already a Black kid has to be lucky to end up in a school system that will prepare her for college, let alone the rigors of law school or medical school. I'm focusing on doctors and medical school, but if you look at the best-paid jobs, they tend to have extensive specialist training. If you do not have the wealth to afford that training, you are entirely dependent on loans and scholarships, and you are in greater competition with all the other students who also need to borrow money to attend. The people who can just afford to pay for their own education have an easier time. Our community is really desperate for professional medical care. This lack of care in the Black community results in poorer outcomes at every level and every age in health. It all comes down to money. We need to be aware of that when we talk about equity. There is no lack of intelligent people who are capable of doing the work. We should have as many professionals (doctors, teachers, lawyers, engineers) as would be proportionate to our population, at least.

This is also true of teachers. Black students do better when they have Black teachers. If you are paying for an education (private or parochial school), you're even less likely to have Black teachers. There are children who go from nursery straight through college and never encounter an instructor who looks like them. That matters. It matters in terms of students feeling that someone is invested in them and their learning outcomes. It matters in terms of their imagination for themselves. Not just for the length of a school year, but for a lifetime in terms of positioning them and helping them to know their value. Those of us who have been lucky enough to have a teacher that opened our minds to the world (shout-out to Carolyn Lumpkin) know that they don't have to be Black to make a difference in our life, but we also know the feeling of teachers who couldn't see us and didn't give a damn about us. For Black students, the person that cares is often a Black teacher. All of these are equity issues. They are economic and historical issues. There is no equity unless we have the resources in our community that can create the same outcomes that other people enjoy.

If our situation was happening in another country, this is the sort of problem the US would send Peace Corps volunteers to address. This is a development issue. We are a resource-starved population, and we need governmental investment to change our educational and health outcomes. And if we were to treat this as a development problem, we would set a national curriculum for every grade, as most countries have, and pay the same amount, per capita, for every student, regardless of their state or neighborhood. It's the only way to make sure that every school educates its children to the highest standard. I think there should be more specific programs to increase the pool of doctors and teachers of color. Pay off their whole student debt if they work for four years in Black communities. If we took these steps, education and health outcomes could improve in a generation. In a country as rich as America, this is an easy fix. We just need to galvanize the political will to make it happen.

I've mentioned that as a result of the video, I've had opportunities to communicate and have very rich experiences with other activists across the world. One of the particularly fruitful and dynamic conversations I've been in has been with Dawn Butler and Clive Lewis, two Black UK members of parliament. At one point, while I was speaking with them about the failings and biases of the US educational system, Lewis said, "It's an educational caste system." He was right, but hearing our educational system described like that was really a punch to the gut because I had never thought of it that way. But once you look at the situation in that context, you can't unsee how big a deal that is.

The US only educates children to the level of the wealth in their environment—which is what happens when local taxes are the primary source of education funding—as opposed to education being considered a right. The government does not think of educating children as the creation of its wealth and its national brain trust, which, for me, would be the wise and appropriate way to think about it. An educational caste system says since you're in the poor caste, we will make it impossible for you to leave your caste. We will reinforce all the social and economic disadvantages of your caste by making sure that educationally you have no access to any opportunities that are not already standard and expected of your caste position. When you put it in those terms, it changes everything. At least it did for me. What suddenly became evident was how this country thinks about the value of young Black minds. How our kids are thought about and positioned is not just a tragedy; it's a crime. It took outsiders reflecting back to me an understanding of a circumstance that of course I know very well in order for me to recognize that it is so much worse than I knew. It is so much more criminal than I understood.

WHAT WE NEED TO DO FOR OURSELVES
BUY BLACK

We have to change the board to change the game, but if we want to win—and by winning, I mean making lives for ourselves that are as big and as healthy and whole as they can possibly be so we can thrive and prosper—we can't just wait for all the help we've earned to arrive. We also have to get our own house in order. In 1862, Frederick Douglass wrote,

> In like manner, we answer those who are perpetually puzzling their brains with questions as to what shall be done with the Negro, "let him alone and mind your own business." If you see him plowing in the open field, leveling the forest, at work with a spade, a rake, a hoe, a pickaxe, or a bill—let him alone; he has a right to work. If you see him on his way to school, with spelling book, geography and arithmetic in his hands—let him alone. Don't shut the door in his face, nor bolt your gates against him; he has a right to learn—let him alone. Don't pass laws to degrade him. If he has a ballot in his hand, and is on his way to the ballot box to deposit his vote for the man whom he thinks will most justly and wisely administer the Government which has the power of life and death over him, as well as others—let

him alone; his right of choice as much deserves respect and protection as your own. If you see him on his way to the church, exercising religious liberty in accordance with this or that religious persuasion—let him alone.—Don't meddle with him, nor trouble yourselves with any questions as to what shall be done with him.

I'm with Fred. If we can even the playing field, we will do just fine. Hell, we've been kicking ass on a field so slanted it might as well be vertical. The very first thing we have to do is keep the Black dollar in the community.

After the looting in Atlanta that led me to record my now-famous video, I was asked if I thought the looting would cause the community to lose the businesses that had set up there. My answer was no. Major corporations and big-box stores know Black people consume like crazy. They are not going to miss the opportunity to sell overpriced whatever to Black people. White people have recognized the value of our dollar. The way we're treated in our own neighborhoods makes it plain that they don't think we deserve the same quality of service people get in other neighborhoods. But they are not trying to miss the opportunity to make money off us. They understand that Black people are a valuable market. But WE haven't understood the value of our dollar.

We have to circulate the Black dollar within the Black community. We have to buy with us. We have to talk about Black businesses in our rap songs instead of white federations that are making money off slave labor in jail. I challenge all the entertainers out there to do a whole album and not mention one company that isn't Black-owned. That's what we need. We don't need any more shooting, killing, disrespecting each other. Uplift your people. If you want to show your strength, uplift your people. Put your people on your back and carry them to the water so that they can liberate themselves. Any rapper that reads this, here's my challenge to you: make your whole next record only shouting out Black-owned swag, what you're drinking, wearing, where you're going . . . Black-owned only. You don't impress us yelling out the names of racist companies that don't give a fuck about your people.

Give your business to shops and services owned by Black people. And when those owners go shopping or need services, we need them to choose other Black businesses wherever they can. When we prioritize buying from each other, and every dollar spent passes from one Black hand to another, and another, and . . . we change the fortunes of our communities. But in order to do this, we need to recognize that we are going to have to give each other some grace.

This is what we do: if you wanted a milkshake from a fast-food chain and every time you go in, the machine is broken, it wouldn't stop you from trying again the next time. And every time you walk through that door, you would return with hope, expecting your shake. But if the machine is still broken, you just buy something else. You don't pass judgment on the entire operation, decide they aren't worth a damn and refuse to ever cross their threshold. You go back again and again, continuing to give them business. We don't offer that same level of grace to Black businesses. Too many of us go into a Black business, and if they don't have what we want or the service is slow, we are ready to pop off, or worse, we get upset about one small thing, go on a Twitter rant and turn off another hundred people from supporting this small Black business.

We are so sensitive to the feeling of being disrespected that we take a small business trying to offer us their best, but maybe not hitting the mark that day, like a slap in the face. Then we go to war against them. And they didn't do anything but make you wait longer than you wanted to. Can we please do better by our sisters and brothers? Can we dig deep and offer our people some of the grace we would love to have for ourselves? The same grace we offer a multibillion-dollar corporation like McDonald's?

One of the ways redlining affects small Black businesses is it makes it difficult for us to get the same lending opportunities our white counterparts get. So many Black businesses begin at a disadvantage. Owners are starting their businesses with their 401(k) or their savings. They are starting a business with a nominal start-up fee, and frequently they don't have a year's worth of payroll and supply money already in the bank, waiting for them to get into the black. That means there might be days where they're paying for things out of pocket. They may need the cash they make one day to pay for the supplies they need the next day. Sometimes things will be short or not right. A restaurant might be short on napkins. They may not have all the silverware. They may have a few things on their menu they are unable to offer. The drink machine may be down.

When we see that situation, we have to know there is heroism going on behind the scenes. If someone is heroically defending their dream of offering a service to me, I want to show up for the love they've put into that dream. I want us all to show up. If you go to a restaurant and they don't have napkins, next time bring them some napkins. Think about the ways you can react that are legitimately and honestly supportive of your brother and sister. And actually do it. Don't just give lip service to "I'm supporting Black businesses." Support goes deeper than spending a nominal amount on an entrée. Ask yourself if you extend grace to a business when it's a little shaky. Are you the person making sure that business thrives and survives? Are you on the 'gram with a photo of your meal telling everyone how good the food is? Even when you had to wait twenty minutes to get it?

This is really about priorities. If you make it a priority to lift your sister and your brother up every time you have the opportunity, you won't just be participating in our economic health; you'll be part of restoring the trust and the collective energy that's been broken with everybody trying to get theirs. Haven't we spent long enough proving to ourselves that we'll get there together or not at all? Why don't we act like we know it? If we can grow the financial power of our communities, if we can get to a place where we are so strong economically, we can afford to create resources in our communities, for ourselves, we can finally change the wealth equation.

And I have to say, one more time, bank with Black banks. When we speak our priorities with the choice to bank with a Black bank, we are demonstrating to the authorities they answer to that there is a commitment to support their existence. The more support they have, the more clout and money they have to invest in the community, whether that means lending for mortgages or small business loans.

SELF-EDUCATION

We know that what it means to be Black in America is to not have as many resources as everybody else, and yet we still have to navigate this world and figure out how we can do better and how we can lift our children and our families up so we can get to being more and having more. We have got to take it as a mission that we are going to educate ourselves. That's going to mean something different to each person, whether that means studying for your GED or thinking about what you would have loved to do if you had gotten the education you deserved and taking yourself back to school to get that education now. Whether that is taking time out of every day to read a book or even just to read the newspaper, we need to be an education community. The truth is, for those of us who went to terrible schools with awful teachers, we don't even know how different education can be. We don't even know how much kids in a rich school system learn every year. We have no idea how many computers and science labs and school trips they benefit from. And we especially don't know how all that money spent by taxpayers on their behalf makes them confident about who they are and what they know. We have to find a way to give that to ourselves if the systems and people charged with our education didn't give it to us.

I started a project on social media where I set a Tuesday Task each week, and everyone is welcome to come learn. All the Tuesday Tasks focus on African American history and offer simple actions to effect change. The goal is for us to learn our history so we can be even prouder of who we are, who came before us and what we've accomplished in America. Whether you're doing the Tuesday Tasks I set, where all you have to do is show up and learn something, or you seek your own learning path, growth is the mission. If you don't have much time, you can get audiobooks from the library to learn some history or science. Learning anything you don't know makes your life bigger. Maybe all you have time for is reading the newspaper while you're sitting on a bus or train on the way home. New information that expands your understanding of the world is education. Educate yourself. Educate yourself. Educate yourself.

We have to educate our kids. There is so much that the internet gives us access to. Too many of us are eating fast food for dinner, but we already know that too much sugar is tied to hyperactivity and kids not being able to focus in school. We already know that kids grow stronger and better when they eat unprocessed foods. Our eating habits are set for our lifetimes in childhood. Depending on where you live, fast food can be cheaper (and faster) than buying groceries and preparing them, but we know what that costs our health as adults. Black people have worse health outcomes than other groups. Part of that has to do with the daily stress we endure, but diet plays a role too. That makes it that much more important that we teach children how to be agents of their own good health.

Watching too much television as a child is tied to poor habits of focus and concentration. We have to set our kids up to succeed. They are growing up in a world that is betting against them, and it's our job to lean hard in the other direction and try to stack the deck in their favor. Everything helps.

We have to educate ourselves so we have the information we need to make healthy choices for our children, and we can make healthier choices for ourselves. The gift we can give our kids is a strong start with good habits. And we have to surround our children with Black excellence. One of the things the white supremacist delusion has enforced, over and over again, is the idea that white people and white culture set the standard for what the world should look like. When kids are watching TV and absorbing all those messages about who is pretty or handsome and who gets to be a hero and how a family behaves, they are being erased from their own minds. We have to put Black people, Black culture, Black beauty and Black power in front of them so they are sure to love themselves. Black children have to be made to feel that they are the point of their own lives.

I was lucky to have a mother who made it her priority to expose us to all kinds of people and experiences that taught us about Black people, our glorious past and who we could be if we took a page from the notes of our powerful ancestors. That made me feel strong and confident about my right to a place in the world, even when I didn't know what I wanted to do or who I wanted to be. Feeling like I could be anything I chose, in the footsteps of all the magnificence that came before me, was like a suit of armor, protecting me as I moved through the world. Give your children some armor.

There are so many people of color writing books for kids that teach them history and lift them up at every age and reading level. You don't have to have money to give your children access to books. Get them a library card. Find a librarian in the kids' section who can help you locate books your child will enjoy. It all takes time, and most of us feel we don't have enough of that, but this is the future we're talking about. We only get to the future we want by getting clear with what we need to do in the present.

In Chicago, I was lucky to have the DuSable Museum and their children's after-school programs. Especially if you're in a big city, there are Black museums and all kinds of cultural resources that have programs for kids. And for adults. It is never too late, and you are never too old to learn something that will make your life bigger. If you're a grandfather, impress your grandkids by taking some night classes to learn something you've always wanted to know. Show them how much education means to you. We need to have education as one of the high, strong values that we hold for ourselves and for our people.

What I want for every one of us is an understanding that we, as a group, are not here by accident. When we learn the history of Black people in America, we understand that everything was done to keep us from getting to the top of the hill. Kids need to know they are not poor because they deserve to be poor. They are poor because the systems around us have impoverished their ancestors and their community. Children are real students of power. They want to have agency for themselves, and they pay attention to those who have it. When a Black child understands that we are here because we did not have the opportunities others were given, and in fact, we were beaten down at every turn, then she can see what America really is. And she can be part of how we get smart, get strong, get skills that pull us out of this situation. Our children need to know their history. They need to know the history of enough exceptional Black folks who found ways to break through anyway, to know that it's possible. And maybe they can be one of those people too. Adults need to know the same things. When we know enough history to look around and see our hand in all of the best of what this country is, we can finally own our place here.

We also need to teach our children economics. They need to understand the importance of their credit, and they need to understand it when they're little. They need to have a dimensional sense of how money and finance work when they're nine and ten, not just when they're teenagers and the world is full of shiny gear they want to buy.

If we are going to have a better future, we have to change what we expect of ourselves and how we engage each other. I've talked about learning our history and the way we teach money and the way we eat. For us to win, we have to learn to protect ourselves. We have to know the law, and we have to fight both within and outside the system. You can't win unless you do both. We might wish we could close ranks and create insular communities that don't have to deal with the government, but that's just a dream. We are still going to have to be organized by the government, whether we vote for those people or not. And since that is the truth of our lives, we have to become active participants and cultivate relationships with the people who govern us. Half of the shit we're in is because of laws made by people who governed us. Laws can be changed, and amendments can be made, but that takes a fight. Fighting for ourselves yields results.

Our ancestors walked 381 days in the Montgomery bus boycott—381 days, with blisters on their feet. For all of the extraordinary work that was done by organizers during the Civil Rights Movement of the 1960s, if the news hadn't covered the atrocities and brutalization, the movement would not have grown, and white people would not have seen the ugliest face of what they stood for when they supported segregation. Whether we're talking about King, X, or any of the Black Panthers, they were eloquent voices of rage and vision, lifted up on our behalf. And if the news had not broadcast them around the world, America would not have been shamed into change. We did not have control of how the story was told, but we were lucky that the importance of our struggle was recognized. What could they have gotten done if they had social media? I love social media because it upends the power dynamic of who gets to control the narrative. The Movement for Black Lives proves that now we don't have to hope to be lucky. We can tell the story ourselves.

The fact that we have this power upsets the power elite, who count on having control of access to the world. It would be easier to maintain white privilege if alternatives were silenced and its ugliest expressions could be suppressed. What social media has done is create real democracy in terms of the transfer of information. I can instantly give you information—vital information—without edits from someone else. Without control from someone else. And even if they take it down, it's been up. Someone has screenshotted it. It may still be circulating. It's very difficult to beat social media because of its speed. Now, information can be transferred around and passed along via social media in a way that is enlightening people. While in the 1960s, people may have only had access to the thirty or forty people that showed up to a basement meeting, now we have the ability to reach thirty thousand in a matter of seconds. Some three million. Some thirty million, all in a matter of seconds. This is power we need to use (responsibly) to find our squad and build our communities.

VOTING

If you're one of the people who thinks your vote doesn't matter, my question to you is: Why are so many people working so hard to suppress it? Why is there gerrymandering, trying to redistrict so even if you do vote, your vote gets washed away in a sea of opposition? Voting is a right a lot of people fought for because they knew how powerful making their choices known could be. But here's the thing: whether you believe me or not, you live in this country and you will live governed by its laws.

Vote, or don't, but elected officials have a direct impact on your life. Wouldn't you rather have a say?

Here in Georgia, the phenomenal Stacey Abrams had an insight that I hope will change this state's politics forever. She realized that the Democrats weren't reaching out to disinvested voters, most of whom were Black, and that if they were to reach those voters who didn't know how valuable their vote could be, the Democrats would win the state every time. The establishment thought they could count us out, until she counted us back in. And in 2020, Democrats delivered the state to Biden and voted two senators to Congress. My point is, votes matter. Voting matters, and if you make it easy for power to deny your vote, you are letting your voice as a citizen be stolen. Is voting the only way we can exercise power? No, but it is the easiest way. It is the way that costs you the least time. *The vote is not your endgame. It's your ticket. It's the beginning, not your end.* It is the minimum standard of how you can show up to advocate for yourself and what's important to you.

Entrepreneur 19Keys says, "Poor people vote, but rich people lobby." That's the history of politics in this country, but I think it's time for us to start lobbying, whether we have the cash to contribute to politicians or not. We need to work with campaigns so officials know us. We need to pool money to get people we trust elected into public office. We need to get to know our city council people and our congresspeople. There are plenty of organizations that focus on electoral politics; get active with one of them.

As passionate as I am about politics and as much as I want to get everybody to vote, this has also been an economic fight. The only people who didn't know they were in it was us. Slavery was an economic decision. The loophole in the Thirteenth

Amendment that created mass incarceration was an economic decision in favor of Southern plantation owners. It looks like politics, but it's always been money. That's why I focus on the economics of the Black community, and that's why the Black dollar plus the vote (and a lot of lobbying) is essential to how we can win.

COMMUNITY AND PERSONAL HEALTH

It is time for us to deal with our trauma. Our ancestors were as smart as (or smarter than) we are, but they lived and raised children in a circumstance where they were treated as though they were just another farm animal, walking on two legs. They were beaten, forced to compete against each other. Forced to turn on each other. Their children were taken. They were "bred"—paired to have sex for the purpose of making bigger, stronger children—whether they loved other people or were traumatized by the process. They watched people they loved be whipped to death or sold away. How does anyone know their power if they can't protect the people they love? How do we learn to function in a family if we can't protect the integrity of that unit? We know how to survive, and we know how to endure, but how do we ever trust that we can build something to last when our experience of slavery and Jim Crow is that anything we valued disappeared in the blink of an eye?

We have been brutalized, traumatized and ridden with generational curses. All of this has affected the way we interact with each other. The grooming systems from slavery are still being taught, by us, to our children. They have impacted the ways we treat each other because of trauma that has been passed down. We have never lived in conditions of enough peace or safety to unwind and heal all the trauma, which has simply

compounded from generation to generation. When we interact with each other in abrasive, aggressive and unloving ways,
that's not natural. That's learned behavior. We need to unlearn
it. During slavery, we didn't have any way to protect our hearts
or those we loved. That's the truth. That's the history, but we
cannot continue to act like it's healthy when we treat each other
badly. It's a health thing at the level of our hearts, but it's a
practical thing at the level of who we have to be if we're going
to walk ourselves out of everything this country did to us.
Obviously, I'm speaking in broad strokes, and there are many
of us who support each other, who love on each other, who
have learned patience and kindness with each other, but that just
means they've healed the top layer of trauma. After four hundred
years, they're not out of the woods either.

It hurts my heart when I see how we actually celebrate the
trauma-rooted mistreatment of each other. We get a kick out
of telling somebody a story about how we cussed somebody
out. We get a kick out of saying how, if this person doesn't do
what we want them to do, we're going to physically harm them.
Potentially even kill them. By doing this we glorify our trauma,
not as a testimony to our pain, but as a testament to who we
are. We've got to stop that shit. Let's start saying, "I choose
to honor my growth and development, and I look at the trau-
mas I inherited and those that have happened in my lifetime as
the story of what I had to grow from." All of this trauma-based
behavior is rooted in slavery, Jim Crow, the crack epidemic, mass
incarceration, the miseducation of the African American child,
police brutality, economic disenfranchisement, poor health,
poor diet. All of this combined affects how we behave and interact with each other.

We are working toward being able to protect each other

instead of harming each other. Instead of being so quick to say, when someone comes to you the wrong way, that you're going to hurt them, we have to learn, among us, to problem-solve. We must be able to resolve conflicts without them becoming fatal. That doesn't mean that we don't need to train and protect ourselves as though we don't have foes. That's protecting ourselves from external sources. But we need to be able to trust each other. We need to know we will not come to harm at our brother's hand. And that's only going to come with healing.

Trauma is a mental health issue. We have to destigmatize mental health concerns. We have to get each other the services we need in order to go on and to grow. And we have to learn how to be nice to each other. In the most simplistic terms, that is it. We have to heal so that we can learn to be nice to each other. Which is why I say, step one is healing. Because if you get the healing under control, then you have the conscious mind to offer each other grace. And then, we can work together to build our economics.

When I see people being so ready to dox each other and cancel each other, that just looks like a symptom of the way this country is mentally ill, and we have all lost our minds. We are all human. We are on a growth journey with each other, and the stupid shit someone might say today could be the door they walk through to become a completely different person, if someone talks with them, instead of canceling them. Where's the road to redemption for people when you cancel them? I think it's inhumane. It doesn't respect the way we learn and grow. And it makes brave people timid and afraid to use their voice. This world is on fire, people. We need all the bravery we can get. Death to cancel culture. Take teachable moments and use them. They're called teachable moments for a reason. Teach!

A teachable moment requires teaching, not cancellation. Not berating. You teach. And you have to give the person the time to learn. To become educated. This is how we vibrate higher. This is how we grow together.

I know cancel culture doesn't seem like it belongs in a conversation about trauma and healing, but the same culture that could treat us like we aren't even human thinks canceling someone is just fine. We have our own trauma to unlearn and heal. We don't need to be adding more to our plate, and we don't need to find new ways to hurt each other.

In the face of our history, healing is a revolutionary act. Healing represents our wholesale rejection of the premise that we are objects "being done to" instead of the point of our own glorious lives. Naming the places where we are not healthy and reaching for health is the choice to move beyond our devastating history. Other communities have better cohesion because they weren't made to distrust each other. Other communities contribute more to their institutions because they feel more connected to the members of their group. When we are healthier, we will love each other better, because we love ourselves better. And that, more than anything, will be a revolution this country can't derail. It's what the Black Panthers were saying decades ago, and it's still true.

In Atlanta, I work with a collective of healers to present a monthly event called Revolutionary Healing. So many people are aware that they need help, but they don't have the money, or they don't trust the medical establishment to give them the help they need. Revolutionary Healing is a free community-based event specifically for people of African and Native American descent. Once a month we offer free yoga, meditation and all types of healing sessions. We have griots that come in to teach.

The most revolutionary thing you can do right now is self-improvement. Healing will allow you to walk and live differently in the space that is called this world and be a better influence on this world. When people tell me they want to be activists, I say, heal yourself. Be better. Be a better model for your children. Be a better model for your friends and family. Heal yourself. Show them what authentic and true healing looks like. It's revolutionary as hell because everyone's afraid to shed that armor. But if you get your courage up and you take that walk, you turn into a change agent who isn't afraid to tell the truth. That's who we have to be to change this country. We have so many healers in the community and so many people who need healing. By working with Revolutionary Healing here, in Atlanta, I see how great the need is.

The very fabulous actress Taraji P. Henson launched a foundation that aims to do a better job of locating mental health resources in the Black community. Only 5.3 percent of psychologists are Black, and that has a real impact on our ability to be seen and heard when we seek help. Named after her father, who struggled with mental health issues, the Boris Lawrence Henson Foundation offers online mental health services and mental health support. She is stepping in to fill a need, and I love that she's doing it. I want to see community-based healing initiatives all over this country. We need it. If you have some skills to offer, begin. Begin in your apartment or at a community center. Begin with some friends, like we did. We need everything. Offer what you've got. Help some folks get better.

I would like to see every one of us in therapy. I want my cousin who looks like a linebacker to be telling me, with tears in his eyes, about the breakthrough he had talking with his therapist. We have to feel like getting the help we need is an act of strength, not weakness. We need to be proud and unashamed of taking care of ourselves. We have to give our kids the language to talk about their fears and their dreams so they can become fearless and dream bigger dreams. Some of us are going to have to learn to open up in ways we have never even seen, but we all know how we wish people would treat us. We need to give that to ourselves, and we need to offer that to each other.

By being a better you, you become a better example to your community. Uplift people whenever you can. Practice patience. And get the services you need. If you have mental health or drug addiction issues, seek help. Do what you can do to get stronger and healthier. Build bridges with the difficult folks in your life. Your healing reverberates and creates healing for many people beyond you.

One of the healing success stories I'm always proud to lift up is the relationship my son's father and I have created. When my son was young, his father and I went to counseling together. We had already broken up, and communication was not good between us, but we were both determined to parent our son well and to figure out how to do that together. We were in counseling for a year, and it was money and time very well spent. It doesn't mean that we always agree, but counseling gave us the tools to engage with each other and a model for how to engage with each other in front of our son. He is a legit partner in raising our son. I know married women who have a partner in the home who wouldn't say that. When I travel, when I'm touring, I never worry. He is in good hands with his father. I'm especially proud of this because we all can have so much distrust and fear that keep us from really coming together in deep and healthy ways.

The goal is for us to know how to love one another. We need to be fluent in compassion and patience and grace. We need to know kindness as strength. Kindness is so gangsta. It takes a really strong person to exercise kindness. Particularly when they haven't necessarily experienced that same level of kindness themselves. There is so much turmoil in this world, and it's easy to be combative. And annoyed. But it takes real work to exercise kindness and to extend each other grace. The journey to healing will be person by person, family by family and community by community. Let's lift our families up with a different vision of how we can handle conflict. Or cultivate peace.

For those of you who have only seen me outraged and ready to tell the truth, I want to make a distinction between the anger that serves us and the anger that can destroy us. I have been called an angry Black woman by people who didn't want to hear anything I was saying (in the video), and damn right, I'm angry. I am angry that Black lives get squandered. Wasted by a dangerous, hateful system that doesn't believe that Black and Brown lives are of equal value to white lives. Anger is the appropriate response to the murderous disregard for my safety and that of others who look like me. I believe that anger is righteous. Hate is destructive, but anger is righteous. We should all have righteous anger when we see injustice. We have to work in love, for ourselves and for each other, but our anger is absolutely appropriate.

With all respect to my ancestors and the brave people who got us to this point, I'm glad to be an activist in this moment when we do not have to support the kind of respectability politics that Martin Luther King Jr. and the nonviolent Civil Rights

Movement had to support in their effort to prove that we were so contained and proper we deserved (by our self-management) to be considered equals—always pressed and in their Sunday best. I have the utmost respect and gratitude to these ancestors and their work, but bullshit to all that. I am equal because I am a human in a world of humans. No one is more valuable than me, and no one is less valuable.

With the truth of our equal humanity established, we have to ask: On what planet, in what war have you ever heard of people asking permission from their oppressor to buck their oppression? So many of you are trying not to be angry because you're worried about the gaze of the oppressor on your rebellion. That is crazy to me. And unhealthy. You are concerned about how you look to your oppressor while you rebel against his oppression? I invite you to feel your anger. Then I invite you to move through it, to work in love. Our healing and our health depend on our ability to feel and communicate with each other. So much has been done to separate us; this is the moment for us to do everything we can to come back together.

NINE PRIORITIES FOR A BALANCED LIFE

Caring for myself is not self-indulgence, it is self-preservation, and that is an act of political warfare.

—AUDRE LORDE

We spend so much time talking about injustices and Black death, we often don't get to speak of life let alone how to live it. While we fight, agitate, ally, educate and vote for justice, we have to live and care for ourselves and each other. This system I'm about to share is one that I have used for a long time. I use it to keep my life in balance and to stay conscious of the values I want to keep front of mind as I make decisions. The busier you are, and the more people you deal with, the easier it becomes to find yourself serving other people's expectations above your own. By having a balanced life, you can be sure that you are expressing your internal priorities and not being dictated to by the world around you.

I have been working on this system since I was nine years old. As a kid, I would look at magazines and try to imagine the lives of the people I saw. I divided life into a few categories, and I would go through the categories, imagining where they were in the different areas of life. Eventually, I started applying the categories to my own life, and the system developed organically as I worked to understand how each of the category elements balanced with each other.

THE NINE PRIORITIES

- Career
- Home
- Transportation
- Relationships
- Finances
- Health and Beauty
- Hobby
- Education
- Community

Each of the areas is an important aspect of our lives, and what I found is that when I'm feeling empty, or lost, or confused, if I write down these nine priorities, and I investigate where I'm feeling weak or strong in each category, I can see where I'm out of balance. So it's a planning tool that shows you how to move forward in your life, but it also works to diagnose what's out of whack and where you're not taking care of yourself.

1. CAREER

Let's start with a distinction. For some of you, there's the job you get paid for . . . and may not enjoy at all. And then there's the thing you're passionate about. The goal is for you to do the work you're passionate about and for that work to be your career.

Now, I'm going to assume you know how you feel about your job. If you don't, you might benefit from paying attention to how you feel on Sunday night when you think about waking up and starting your work week. I have a friend who loves to clean. It's not how most people want to spend their time, but she loves it. Cleaning allows her to zone out and think. She loves bringing order to chaos. She loves the feeling she has when she looks at an orderly and spotless space and can say, "I did that." So cleaning is her passion, and she has contracts with the City of Atlanta. That's the other part. Being passionate about cleaning, she has risen in her capacity and her level of expertise to being an expert. So she is well paid and successful at something she loves. So many people are daydreaming at work, trying to make their jobs bearable by escaping their actual situation. But for her, she goes to work and escapes *into* her work. That's the goal for each of us.

If you are not excited about the work you are being paid to do, Career is the place for you to focus on. We spend more time at work than any other space in our lives. If you are not happy with your work, it's hard to be happy in the other areas of your life. If you don't already know, you have to do the work to discover what you're passionate about doing. And then you have to find a way to make the transition into doing that meaningful work as your career. To be clear, I'm not telling you to quit your job and start a business. But if there's a way to supplement the job you do with some work you love, begin doing that.

When I was a fledgling writer, I was absolutely clear on writing as my destination, but I didn't know where or how to start. There are online groups for everything. I learned so much from the writing communities on Facebook. People posted advice, job opportunities and all kinds of freelance gigs that give you something to put on your résumé and get you comfortable with calling yourself a writer. That was my experience, but there are virtual communities for all kinds of work. If you want to be an interior designer or work with animals or . . . whatever, there's probably a group where people are exchanging ideas and teaching each other the ropes. And if an online platform doesn't have a specific group for astronaut florists who arrange moonflowers, or whatever most interests you, you will surely find your squad somewhere on the internet. Join groups, find your community any way you can and begin to grow your skills and your network. Once you achieve a professional level at the work you're passionate about, you can use the network you've developed to start looking for work. I really believe in creating financial security for yourself (as you'll see when we get to Finances), so I would never tell you to risk the work that's paying your rent and feeding you, but when you reliably have as much work doing your passion as you need to support yourself, jump into it. I'll be here cheering for you.

2. HOME

Home is a big one because it should be your safe space where you can dream and grow and nurture your ideas. Ideally, your home should be your happy oasis away from the world. It doesn't matter if you're living in a converted garage or a mansion, it should be your castle. If you haven't been treating your home like a castle, the first thing I want you to do is take $20—or less—out of your budget for the month (we'll get to your budget) and buy some small things to fluff up your environment that reflect your style and your tastes. It can be some small candles or maybe pillows or some fabric to add some color somewhere in your home. You think about the clothes you wear when you present yourself to the world. Dress your home up in whatever expresses warmth and comfort to you.

This next part is important. If there is someone in your home who keeps you from having your peace, it is time to figure out a transition plan to get them out of your home. That may sound harsh, but having comfort and peace in your home is paramount. Our lives demand too much of us. Insist on being able to fully relax and recharge where you live.

Now, if you do not have a space of your own and are in a position I call "safe homelessness," meaning that you're living with a friend or family member, but it isn't your own space, and you are reminded of that fact often as you move through the space, call 211. It is a great resource for many different needs. The number is national, but the resources and recommendations are local. If you are in Illinois and you call 211, you will get information and help for the county you're in, in Illinois. You will speak with someone who will be knowledgeable about the resources in your area; 211 provides services that apply to some of the other priorities as well. This won't be the last time I refer to it.

If you are in the condition of safe or unsafe homelessness, call 211. They will ask you what services you need, and you will tell them your issue is homelessness, and you would like help from all the services and programs relevant to your situation. Once, when I needed help, I was helped by Travelers Aid. There are a few Travelers Aid programs across the country, but not all of them help to get people housed, as the one in Atlanta does. And again, I probably found my way to Travelers Aid after calling 211. The website www.rentassistance.us allows you to search by zip code to locate agencies that might be able to help you.

I want to say a word about participating in services like the ones 211 offers. Black people have been impoverished and under-educated since our feet touched land in this country. The same people who have denied us access and livelihood have tried to heap shame on us for not having gotten further in their rigged system. If you need help, ask for it. We seem not to understand that the programs and resources that are designed to support us at our lowest are entitlements. They are programs that our tax dollars have been paying into since our first paycheck at our first job. I'm not saying it's free money. I'm saying the help comes from money you already paid. If you need to ask for some of it back, in the form of assistance, do that. And know it's just another step on your journey through a system that was not designed for you to succeed. I'm betting on you anyway. But the system isn't helping. Unless you specifically ask for help.

3. TRANSPORTATION

The third principle of a balanced life is Transportation. Some of you live in cities where you don't need a car and have already decided you don't need to think about transportation. But I'm not just talking about having and maintaining a car. Transportation is all about your being able to move the way you need to move. How you need to move will depend on where you are and who you are. This section is about making sure you are organized to meet your own transportation needs.

Having a full and balanced life means being able to partic-ipate in all the areas represented by the other priorities. If you need a car and have the funds to buy a car, I recommend you go ahead and do so. If you don't need a car where you live, but you need another form of reliable transportation, I suggest you make a commitment to having other forms of transportation available to you. That might mean committing to a monthly metro pass so you can take a subway or bus without having to think about it or plan for it. Just knowing your ability to move is assured opens you up to more engagement with the world around you.

If your current situation is that you don't have the money or the stability to make a commitment to regular transportation, I am again recommending you call 211. In this case, 211 might be able to secure a free or discounted bus pass for you. Most transit systems have discounts for students or the elderly or for people with disabilities.

For those of you who can afford to have a car, I want you to focus on maintenance. This means regular oil changes, tune-ups and tire rotations. Recognize the importance of having reliable transportation, and treat your car like you know how important it is. I also want to point out that if you have a perfectly adequate car, but you're dreaming of something better, at every price point, maintaining a car gets more complex and more expensive. If you're not taking good care of the Toyota that you could drive until its wheels fall off, you're going to ruin a Mercedes, which requires more attention. Get in the habit of taking care of whatever you have. Even if, right now, it's just a bus pass.

4. RELATIONSHIPS

This is the biggest and the most complex of the priorities. There are so many different ways we interact with the people in our lives. The goal of simplifying the way we think about our relationships is to make sure we are taking care of ourselves, first and foremost. This doesn't diminish the importance of the people you love and their place in your life; it just makes sure that by staying present to what you want and need for yourself, you are able to offer the best version of yourself to them when you engage.

This priority has five subcategories. They are:

- Spirituality
- Spouse/Significant Other
- Family
- BFF
- Business Associates

SPIRITUALITY

For me, that's God. I'm not a religious person, but I do believe in God. Spirituality is personal. It's the most individually wrapped thing in the world—as individually wrapped as humankind itself. For me it's really about trusting that there's a larger plan working for my good. Every path that I've been on that has enriched my life and others' was unplanned—even becoming an author. I was a screenwriter but I had no real designs of being a novelist. Getting that job at Little Shop of Stories returned me to literature in a more profound way. None of that stuff was planned, so it's difficult for me to believe that there isn't a great plan in life. This even applies to my son, who is my super miracle baby, and he's brilliant. (I know everybody thinks their baby, is brilliant, but my baby IS brilliant.) He was born six weeks early and there is nothing wrong with that kid other than a little eczema. I have a strong belief in prayer and I meditate every other day. Sometimes as short as two minutes, other times as long as an hour. It centers me; it calms me. I find that when I mediate at the top of the morning I am a lot less emotionally moved by any trials and tribulations that come forth in the course of the day. I can't allow myself to be moved by every reaction to me or every occurrence in the world. If I am derailed by everything that happens in the world, then I can't do good work or practice good leadership.

Maybe you already have a spiritual or faith practice. Maybe you don't, but you believe that we are innately good, and you practice kindness as your way to participate in the positive energy of the world. Whatever spirituality means to you, tap into it every day.

SPOUSE/SIGNIFICANT OTHER

This one is super, super-duper-duper, super-super-duper import-ant. I know some people will resist this, but if you are being authentic and honest with yourself, you recognize the truth of it. Romantic love is the most influential love in your life. For those of you who feel like your children are your big love, I don't doubt the love, but instead I would say that they are your most developmental love. You and your child(ren) are involved in a two-way, mutual development project. You are develop-ing them, and you are developing a better form of yourself as a model for them. But romantic love has the most influential effect on you.

I'm not making a distinction here about being married or not. Any person who you are in a committed, long-term romantic relationship with, regardless of how that relationship is defined, will have the most influence on your daily activities. Especially if you live together.

This is your ultimate deal, and it is where you have to make sure you choose well. Attraction plays a part in your choice, but it should not be the most important consideration. You need to be clear about your standards for a partnership. You need to know what you offer but also what you expect. And you need to be honest with yourself about whether your needs are being met. Your significant other is either going to be your blow up and glow up or your downfall and dismay.

You want to choose someone who is compatible with all the aspects of your life. If you are a person who likes to hit the road and travel every five minutes, you cannot be with someone who does not like to travel. After a while it's probably going to cause drama in your house. And now we're back to the principle of home and the peace you want to cultivate and protect in your home environment. Your peaceful home will be disrupted by the wrong significant other. If they aren't your peace, they are your chaos.

Many of us have had negative experiences in relationships and have chosen to protect our independence in future relationships, not wanting to repeat the experience. But denying the importance and the influence of your romantic relationship only turns the relationship into a struggle. Understand this: relationships are a deal. Decide what you need from a romantic partner to allow them fully into your life. Decide who you need a romantic partner to be to allow them to be an influence in your life. Know your own deal. If the person you are with does not satisfy the terms of your deal, you can't be with them. If you don't trust their decision-making, based on watching how they organize their own life, you don't trust the decisions they will make in yours. You need to be with someone you feel you could trust with your whole life. Do you have that level of trust in your own relationship partner? If the answer is yes, you have something worth working on and fighting for. If the answer is no, you shouldn't trust that person to influence you. Which they will, whether you recognize them or not as your significant other.

Here's another way to think about it. Looking at the objective facts, if you were to think of being a romantic partner as a job and you gave your significant other a job review, would you give them a raise? Would you demote them? Fire them? If they need to be fired, let them go. Hell, if they are just punching the clock, let them go. Choose an influence you can trust and who is earning their promotions.

FAMILY

Family is a difficult one because some family members mean us no good. Set boundaries with them. If they are a tornado in your house, you can love them with a long-handled spoon. You will see them at the family reunions, at the funerals, at the weddings and at a cookout, but put them on "do not disturb" on your phone. Your peace is a nonnegotiable. We don't get to choose our family, but we can most certainly choose which of them we interact with. I don't care if it's your mama. If she's an agent of chaos, limit her ability to affect you.

BFF

Notice I did not say "friends," plural. I am only talking about your best friend. Your best friend should be the person who supports you. The person who is not an agent of chaos but an agent of calm in your life. The person who has been there for you, through thick and thin. The person who makes you laugh.

The person who, when something exciting happens in your life, you pick up that phone and call them. The person that when the day is bad, you just want to talk to them. A person who knows your kids well. This person who is your true blue, ride or die. That's the person you commit to and give your energy to. But for your own peace and your time management, choose only one. One person who you love and for whom you will reliably feel obligated to show up.

This friend is the one person that, when you're tired and you don't feel like leaving the house, you get up and go to their event anyway. One person who, even though you're in a rut, when they're trying to get you to go out to dinner, you get up and do it. Choose one person who has earned your time and attention. If you choose more than one person, you'll never be able to balance all of the rest of the priorities. Once you've chosen your one person, your time with everyone else is negotiable. If you don't feel like doing what they want you to do, "no" is a full-stop sentence.

BUSINESS ASSOCIATES

Do not treat business associates like friends. They are business associates. You are in business with them. Of course, you can be friendly, but they are not your friend, and knowing that, have boundaries in your business relationships. Do not involve them in your personal business with your spouse or your best friend or your family.

Stay aware of the value a business associate brings to your professional life. If you don't feel there is forward motion in your work with a business associate within an eighteen-month period, let them go. You have to be a timekeeper. Your time is exceptionally valuable, and it's your job to review how you spend your time and decide if everyone is worthy of it. Treat your time like currency. You are paying time to people. Who's worthy of that time?

YOUR PHONE

Now, here's my homework for you. On whatever kind of smartphone you have, you can designate certain people as your "favorites." You're going to use nine spaces (if you use ten, you're already committing to doing too much). Choose nine favorites based on the Relationship principles.

Spiritual adviser: choose one person who represents your commitment to your spirituality. If you worship with other people, maybe this space will be filled by your imam or the deaconess from your church. It could be the auntie who prays for you. Or a person who counsels you. If they represent your spiritual space, put them at the top. You're going to honor that connection by putting them where you can get to them quickly.

Significant Other: the person in the number two spot will be your significant other. If you don't have one, you are only going to have eight favorites on your phone. For my single people who are out there dating, you are not going to give that spot to anyone until they earn it. Write down everything you expect from a relationship. Get clear on what is required to have you as a spouse, because you are a gift. When someone shows up who is worthy of that space, you will add them to your favorites.

Family: you get four family spots. In my phone, my mother, my son and two of my siblings are my four. Think about your closest family members and choose the four who support you and represent peace in your life. These have to be four people you never mind talking to.

BFF: a spot for your bestie.

Business Associates: you will use two spaces for your business associates. In your professional life, you may be obligated to speak to many people every day. But choose two people with whom communication is part of the forward motion of your professional life. In my case, these two spots are filled by my assistant and my agent. I have a lawyer and other people I need to be in contact with, but my assistant and agent are the two I have the most contact with, so they're the ones on speed dial. If you have a coworker or a direct report who you communicate a lot with, they will get one of the two spots. If you have a business partner, they will have a spot.

That's your nine. I know some of you feel you have more than one best friend. Choose one. If you're honest, you know that you feel closer to one. That's the one on speed dial. The reason you only get to put these slots in your phone is because on a daily basis, when you are getting ready to randomly scroll through your phone and call or text people, you call from that list. You go to that favorites list, and you communicate with somebody on that list. You do this for multiple reasons. If you curated the list properly, these are the people who warrant your time. And time is currency. These are also the people that you need to check on and check in with. These are the people who reciprocate. These are also the people who keep your life in forward motion. What you don't want is partial influence from people who don't matter. If you're getting advice about work, if you're getting advice about what to do with your child, all you need to do is scroll through your list. These are your trusted confidantes. And people, stop telling your business to everybody outside of your list of trusted confidantes.

I think this is the most important section of the priorities. You are going to curate your relationships. You are going to pay attention to who you communicate with and stay aware of the quality of the influences in your life. Do not allow outside forces that do not serve you to be in your head embedding thoughts. Choose wisely and choose people who continue to earn that space you give them.

5. FINANCES

Finances impact everything. How does money affect your relationships? Well, have you ever yelled at your child for telling you at the last minute about something he needs, when the truth is you are just frustrated because getting what he needs will put a financial strain on you? You understand that a ten-year-old forgets sometimes, but now you find yourself chastising your child. If this is what's happening in your life, your financial house isn't in order. Money is the number one stressor in our lives. It's the number one cause of divorce. It is the difference between equality and equity. It is the difference between being able to fight the system of injustice and not. It's what you need to provide the elements in the other priorities. Too many people think they have to earn Elon Musk–style money to save anything. But people who build wealth know that it isn't about a big paycheck. It's having a plan and a system for how you think about and organize your money that makes the difference. And this is one of the things that most Black people don't know. This lack of financial literacy is a result of the ways in which we have been denied the possibility of generational wealth. Many of us have never even met a person who is financially secure, and we don't know what those people know. We don't have access to those people to ask questions and learn what they know.

The system I'm going to explain has worked for me. If you read any book about saving money, it all comes down to the same thing: make a budget, divide your funds into categories and protect those categories so you can see real progress toward your goals. But also set aside some bucks for fun because if you don't, you'll be like those dieters who only eat celery for a week, then eat a whole chocolate layer cake in a half hour when they get so tired of denying themselves something that could make them happy. Saving money is a discipline. It can be hard to start, but when you see the numbers growing in your account, it will make you proud of yourself and keep you going.

Again, I'm going to send you to my favorite folks at 211. They can direct you to services that help you to repair your credit. That help you with saving, and that help you with home buying. With money you can see the interconnectivity of all the priorities. There is nothing wrong with renting if that's the money you have, but if you get your credit straight and you save some money, you become able to buy a place of your own. You don't want to buy a home if you don't have what you need to maintain it, but as I've said and I'll keep saying, homeownership is the first step toward generational wealth. And generational wealth is the key to long-term financial success in a capitalist system. So you'll call my friends at 211 and they can direct you to help for first-time home buyers, which will help you prepare for homeownership with a six- to eighteen-month preparedness program.

And here's something else: I want us to stop being afraid and ashamed to take advantage of services. Rich people take advantage of all the services that are available to them, all the time. How do you think they get the bailouts we are so sick of seeing

them receive? They understand how to use government programs for their own benefit. And they understand that they've
been paying taxes into the capitalist system and earning the
right to access the programs that are available to them. We
have been shamed so often for any little crumbs we have been
given in a system that is dedicated to keeping us poor and power-
less that now we're hesitant to ask for anything because we
expect some type of stigma if we get any help. We have got to
get over that. Everybody's leaping forward while we're inching
along, too embarrassed to get help. No one's embarrassed but us.
Let's get over that now.

YOUR CHILDREN

Each of your children should have a 529 college fund. In
today's world, it is very hard to make a living wage without a
college degree, and yet debt for college is the greatest debt we
put on young people as they start their lives. This is yet another
place where it makes a big difference that we don't have generational wealth. Until we all have homes and property and
something enduring to pass down to our kids, make sure every
child in your life has a 529.

There will be a minimum. In Georgia, where I live, I have
to put $30 in every month to maintain the 529. When it's time
for your child to go to college, there will already be money in
the 529. Depending on how much the school costs, maybe your
child won't have to take out a single loan. It will lessen the burden, in any case.

PEOPLE, BE SMART. GET THAT DEBT OFF YOUR
BABIES. Every child should have a 529 from the day they
are born. If you're an auntie or an uncle, take care of the kids
in your life by organizing these resources for them. Give them

some financial freedom so they can make the choice that we couldn't make when we had to start servicing our student debt six months after we graduated.

LIFE INSURANCE

Get life insurance. Even if you can't afford a big policy, get whatever you can afford. Your family should not have to do a GoFundMe to pay for your funeral when you go. Plan ahead. Make things easier for the people you love.

If you can afford a larger plan, the ideal use of life insurance is that it will fill in the gaps you leave for the people you love. If you are the primary wage earner in your family, the goal would be for insurance to keep your family living at the same standard in your absence. Think about the financial impact of each family member if they go and get a policy proportionate to what that impact would be.

IRA

You need an Individual Retirement Account, better known as an IRA. There is no guarantee that Social Security will still be around by the time we stop working. An IRA is another way to save for retirement. If you're lucky, you'll get Social Security and an IRA when you retire, but make sure you'll have some income to support yourself with. Even if all you can afford is $10 a month, start. Do something and get used to thinking of your future and the elements you need in place to have resources throughout the length of your life.

Here's how an IRA works: banks and other financial institutions such as investment companies offer these accounts, which allow you to earn tax-deferred growth on funds invested strictly for retirement. If you don't have friends who are happy about the way their IRA is growing, you could talk to a financial planner or you can look online to get reviews of the different companies that offer them and choose that way. Once you have chosen a company to work with, you'll open an IRA with them and choose an amount that will be transferred into your account every month. As I said, it can be as little as $10 a month. It you're under fifty years old, you can put in as much as $6,000 a year. You can put in $7,000 a year if you're over fifty. You might want to get some advice for the next part. You will choose what type of fund to put your IRA in. If you're young and you still have time to watch the market dive and recover a few times, you can afford to put your money in an aggressive fund that will invest in some places where the outcome might not be assured. But if you're over fifty and you want to make sure you are never at risk of losing money, you might choose a low-risk plan. The point is, there are all kinds of plans and you can choose the one that will serve you best.

I learned how to organize my money from Thad Gilliam, a good friend of mine. Thad is a financial planner and what I share here is some of what I learned from him.

YOUR ACCOUNTS

You will need five different bank accounts. They are:

- Checking
- Savings
- Fun
- Vacation
- Emergency

These accounts are in addition to the 529s you're paying into for your children, the IRA you're adding to for your retirement and maybe a monthly payment to maintain your insurance. This is important: you should always be paying more into your retirement than you are paying into your child's 529. If your funds are limited and you have to choose, your retirement has priority. In the worst case, your child will be able to get scholarships and loans for college. You want to save your kid from uncertainty, but you know there will be money for college, even if it creates debt. At the same time, you have to make sure you do not become a burden to your child in your senior years. You want to allow them to live their lives and spend their money on their kids' Disney World trip instead of taking care of your hip replacement. At some point, you will also need to organize long-term care insurance for yourself, which means that if your kids have to put you in the back room with a nurse, your long-term care insurance will cover that, and they won't have to.

Fun Account

The fun account is my favorite. In your budget, you include a line for FUN. This is just loose, willy-nilly money. It's for going out to dinner with friends. It's money for the movies, going to play Topgolf. You should already have a line in your budget for clothing, so clothing is not included in fun. Fun is for buying something like lip gloss, if you love lip gloss. If you're like me and you live for eyelashes, they come out of the fun account. And when the money in your fun account is gone, it's gone. That's it. No more fun for you this month.

If you put money in your fun account at the beginning of the month but spent it all, and now your girlfriends say, "We are all going out on the twentieth," would you think, I want people to think I don't have money? I need to be flexing for the 'gram. I gotta let them know I'm ballin'. Or would you model some good financial behavior for your friends and say, "I really want to go with you, but you know how I do. I got my fun account and it's depleted. So, no more fun with a price tag for this month. Now, if one of y'all want to pay my way, that's dope. I'll show up then. Otherwise, I'll catch you next month." You get a certain amount of fun every month that you can blow on whatever. When the fun money is gone, you better play some puzzles at home and watch some Netflix or go to the park. All your fun has to be free after that.

Vacation Account

This one is self-explanatory. I don't care if you are just going to your auntie's house. Get out of your regular and see something different. It's good for the soul. It's educational for your kids. It's good for your spirit to relax, so put some money in your vacation account.

Savings Account

You save and you just keep adding to this account, watching your money grow. You never touch it. This is the money you use for your retirement, or if you make a big purchase, like a home. That's what savings are for.

Emergency Account

Your emergency account is NOT your savings. This is your rainy-day money for when unexpected things happen. A tire goes out on your car. Your favorite cousin, who made it onto your family list in your phone, goes to jail and you have to bail him out. A bill came up that you had forgotten about. You were on vacation and your child ate up all the snacks in their hotel room and now that food has been charged to your account by the hotel, so you need to supplement the money that was taken out. You're going to transfer money from the emergency account. It is for emergencies. If you need emergency surgery, but you've got to pay a $500 deductible upfront, that money comes out of your emergency account. You have the emergency account so you don't have to take money out of your general savings for emergencies.

Each of you will figure out the best way to organize your accounts. I suggest your checking and savings accounts be linked—in the same bank, sharing a bank card—but you might make a different choice. I think your fun account needs its own card, so you can't accidentally (on purpose) spend more than you've put in the account. I prefer that the vacation and emergency accounts be digital accounts so that the money needs to be transferred when you need it, not just accessed with a card.

If you have a partner and you pool your money, it's going to make sense to have joint vacation and savings/checking accounts, but your fun account should be all yours. You and your significant other should each have an account of your own. Maybe when you go out together, you can take turns paying. Figure that out in whatever way works for you both.

BTW, find the Black-owned bank in your area. There's also Greenwood Bank, a young online bank that's Black-owned. I talk a lot about circulating the Black dollar, so of course I have an account. I'm recommending Black-owned financial institutions to everyone who will listen because it's a big step in the direction we need to be traveling.

6. HEALTH AND BEAUTY

This priority is all about your body. Are you eating well? Exercising? Health and Beauty is about the obvious stuff, but it's also about making sure you have health insurance. And making sure you look and feel fly. Your appearance is an expression of your personality and self-expression is important.

In this day and age, health should be a human right. But it isn't yet, so you have to get some health insurance. If you have missed the window for Obamacare, see if you qualify for Medicaid. Definitely sign up for health insurance if your job provides it. And if all else fails, every county hospital has a sliding-scale health program. You will have to show proof of your income in order to receive medical services based on what you can afford. Not just in the emergency room but affiliate doctors that you can go see in optometry, dental, family care, general practice . . . and you can see them on a sliding scale based on your income.

Historically, Black people don't see doctors regularly, and we wait so long to see a doctor when something goes wrong that we are more likely to be seriously ill when we finally get help. By creating an infrastructure for your health, you can be both proactive and reactive. Not just one or the other. Pay attention to your body, have a routine of seeing your doctors and stay on top of your health concerns.

And people, everybody, literally EVERY BODY, needs to get some mental health services. We have all been battered and bruised by life. Some of us to a greater degree than others. But at the end of the day, the bottom line is: we have all lived, and in living, you are going to get scarred. Start putting some mental Neosporin on those scars. If you feel you can't afford it, call my favorite number, 211. They will tell you where you can get free or sliding-scale mental health services.

One last note for health and beauty: eat better. You are what you eat. If you eat shit, you are going to feel like shit. You eat well, so you can feel well and look well.

7. HOBBY

The point of a hobby is for you to have something that you enjoy doing that takes your mind away from the day-to-day bustle of the world. It can be anything. Collecting stamps, knitting, travel. Some people are great musicians and they just want to play in a café on Saturday nights to heal their soul, but they love their day job as an accountant, so it's their hobby. I have a few hobbies. For example, I love plants and have so many in my home. The crazy thing is that I don't really have a green thumb (a lot of my plants don't make it), but tending to plants relaxes me. When I find that one of my beloved plant children has root rot, or has grown and needs repotting, having to move the soil is so soothing. You can have as many hobbies as you want, as long as only one of them costs you money. If you have more than one hobby, the others have to pay for themselves. We are trying to get into financial balance, so your hobbies cannot be how you go broke.

When you feel unbalanced, it's usually because you are not doing enough of what you enjoy. Your hobby should be something that feeds your heart. If you feel better when you're doing your hobby, it's a good choice for you. Feed your heart.

The hobby you choose may depend on the money you have. If you're a foodie and love buying the best ingredients to cook with, or going to the finest restaurants to taste the food of other chefs is your heart's desire, save up your fun money and make it happen. The point is your hobby should take you to your happy place. It should be a tool you have to take care of yourself. If you are unhappy and sewing puts you in your happy place, then get out your machine and make something. Think about what makes you feel good and claim it as your hobby.

8. EDUCATION

Education is not just academic education in school. Academic education may be an important part of you getting ahead or realizing your dreams. Go for it. But as I said earlier, self-education is also important. Real education, regardless of where you get it, makes you better at understanding the world you live in and understanding yourself in the world. It gives you discernment so you don't just fall for any old thing.

Unfortunately, a lot of people want to appear knowledgeable, but they aren't doing the work to know what they should know. Whatever you care about, you should constantly be educating yourself on the subject. One time I met with a young aspiring filmmaker and they asked me things they could have learned from any book. They could have found the answers online. They wasted their time and mine. Educate yourself so you know where resources for information are. Educate yourself so you ask better questions when you have access to a resource that isn't usually available to you. You should be reading all the time. Going to the library or ordering books (from independent booksellers, please) all the time. Education is elevation.

9. COMMUNITY

Do something for somebody else. Period. There are lots of people doing good work that can benefit from your money or need you to volunteer to help in any way you can. Volunteer at your child's school. Do some volunteer work through your faith organizations. Do something. Organize. If you have made it out of your hood and now you're living well in the suburbs, organize a community cleanup in your old hood so other people can experience their environment the way you experience yours now. Our communities need so much. It is not hard to figure out where you might be able to lend a hand.

It is critical that you give back. You can do it within your family. Are you the family member everybody borrows money from? If you are a Simpson, you can create the Simpson Family Fund. Add a line to your budget that says, "I'm going to loan five hundred dollars a month to family members. And I'm going to have that fund be run by my cousin Tamika." Choose the cousin who is organized and who no one wants to mess with. The one everybody knows will cuss them out if you push her buttons. You can set up the fund for an auto-transfer every month. When family members need to borrow, they can fill out a form online and Tamika will make sure she handles it. Once the $500 is gone, nobody else in the family can borrow money from you. That's giving back. That's your family. Your family is your community.

It's essential to have some kind of community service to balance out your life. That's how we impact this world and make this a better place. Everybody's going to do their thing. And you only have to do your thing. You're not responsible for taking up all the fights and all the plights. But know what your fight and your plight is, and go hard for it. If you're big on education, then you need to be working with some lobbying groups to get adjustments made in education. If you're concerned about local politics, then there are task forces and organizations to join and participate in.

Now that we've moved through all the priorities, get a little notebook, write down all of the priorities and assess where you are with each of them. Keep referring to the notebook and when you feel off-balance, and use the priorities to see what you're not doing so you can set yourself straight. Maybe you'll discover that you haven't been giving your hobbies any time, and that explains your stress. Or that you haven't been helping in your community and that's why you feel disconnected. Let the balance the priorities offer be a map to greater health and purpose in your life.

HOPE LOOKS LIKE THE FUTURE

May 2021 marked one hundred years since the infamous 1921 massacre in Tulsa, in which white mobs unleashed violence against the city's Black people, Black institutions and Black wealth. An estimated three hundred people were killed, and approximately thirty-five acres of commercial and residential property within the Greenwood district—known as Black Wall Street—were destroyed. With six hundred Black-owned businesses, the community was exactly what I mean when I speak of circulating the Black dollar. The Tulsa massacre has not been taught in schools and has only recently begun being discussed nationally. The civil unrest of 2020 opened a floodgate of white Americans pulling the veil from in front of their implicit biases and their taught white-nationalist fantasy land. Tulsa was one of the collective truths they were forced to face.

According to a 2001 report by the Oklahoma Commission to Study the Tulsa Race Riot of 1921, at least 1,256 homes were destroyed, alongside churches, schools, businesses and hospitals.

Greenwood residents would go on to file over $1.8 million in damage claims; in today's dollars, this would be over $27 million. All but one of these claims were denied: a white shop owner was given compensation for guns taken from his shop. The report acknowledges, however, that not all residents took out insurance or filed claims.

As I wrote this, a McKinsey & Co. report estimated "a $330 billion disparity between Black and white families in the annual flow of new wealth, some 60 percent of which comes from intergenerational transfers. Every year there is a massive intergenerational transfer of family wealth, creating an effect that is both profound and self-perpetuating. Black families are less likely to receive inheritances, and when they do, the amounts are smaller. The gap in inheritances between Black and white recipients is some $200 billion annually."

What would that look like for our community now if we had been able to sustain that generational wealth? Not just in Tulsa, though; in all the areas that similar atrocities occurred. The number is in the dozens—and that's just the documented ones. Couple that with the Freedman's Bank tragedy, the collapse of the Freedmen's Bureau and the removal of people from their given land, and there's no way to calculate the loss of generational wealth for Black Americans at the hand of the white supremacist delusion. A debt is owed.

In April 2021, on the day the verdicts on charges for the murder of George Floyd came in, I went live on social media to watch with the activist community and followers I'd come to know over the past year. Derek Chauvin was found guilty on all three counts: second-degree murder, third-degree murder and manslaughter. I jumped out of my seat and shed tears when the judge asked the jurors, "Are these your true and correct verdicts?" and they all answered, "Yes." Outside, people were cheering in the streets. Before I headed out to join them I clapped in my living room. I said to the folks watching: "Let's go! We outside, but we outside to celebrate. Bring your drums, your tambourines, let's go! And after this let's start planning. This is not a time to stop, this is a time to start. Apply pressure! We been applying pressure since Trayvon. We been applying pressure since Rodney King. We been applying pressure since John Lewis. We been applying pressure since Emmett Till. The people needed a win and they got it today, but this is the beginning of the work. The beginning of the work. Now the people, take your power back, and let's do for self. We outside, but we outside to celebrate, to prepare, to shift. Win one of a million. This has to be win one of a million because we still need justice for Rayshard Brooks, we still need justice for Daunte Wright, we still need justice for Adam Toledo. We still need justice for Jamarion Robinson, for Jimmy Atkinson, for Vincent Truitt. I know some of them names y'all don't even know. This is win one. Win one of a million."

What that verdict offered, first of all, was justice. George Floyd's life could not be returned, but his murder was recognized and punished for what it was, which is all too often not the case—as we saw when no officers were charged for Breonna Taylor's death. The second thing it offered was hope. Between the COVID-19 pandemic and the continued brutality against Black and Brown bodies, people were feeling an extreme sense of loss without any semblance of the needle moving. Lots of folks had raised their voices, but since Floyd's death almost a year earlier, not enough time had passed for institutions to show us that they were sincere. This verdict was evidence of the needle moving. It is so unfortunate that in the midst of it, people had to experience trauma again. I was in the streets celebrating the verdict when a call came in telling me about the murder of a young sister. Ma'Khia Bryant's tragic death is proof that the work is never-ending. I don't know what the end of this fight looks like; I just know it's not now.

I love the phrase from the Civil Rights Era, "None of us are free until all of us are free." Even if America became a perfect utopia, it would still be unacceptable for me to not worry about my brothers and sisters in the rest of the world. It's not about hopelessness. It's not that. I understand that the work continues as long as the work exists. And with that understanding, I don't get frustrated. I understand that the work is massive. That the white supremacist delusion is entrenched. Really, what we need is growth from every human being now and to come. Personal growth is revolutionary. Imagine if every person woke up and said, "I'm going to work to be better: a better participant, better at grappling with childhood trauma, to do the work of combating implicit bias, to be a better listener." Imagine if everybody did just that . . .

After four centuries, Black people have finally learned that the racism of the dominant culture is not our problem. It is a psychological illness, and we cannot cure the delusions of grandeur and supremacy inherent in the delusion because we have done nothing to create or support it. It is uniquely a problem white people have to solve on their own. It's heartening to see so many people coming out of the delusion, and I can only imagine that as the fever breaks and the scales fall away from people's eyes, there will be less resistance and more possibility to work together to craft a better version of this country.

For most Black people, it's been a relief to recognize that racism is not our business. In our time on American soil, we have believed that if we could just be exceptional or persuasive enough, our value would be indisputable, and we would be given enough space to find our footing. Now we are clear that the fight we are in is economic. It was never about our value or our dignity; it was always, only, about resources and access to power. And that frees us to take our emotions out of the equation. This is not a heart fight; it's a head fight.

Fred Hampton, who was the chairman of the Illinois chapter of the Black Panther Party until he was assassinated in 1969, is a real hero of mine. He said, "We're going to fight racism not with racism, but we're going to fight it with solidarity," and I think that's the best thing we can do. In the face of the extrajudicial killing spree law enforcement has been on, we are making noise and letting everyone know that we are not going anywhere. This must stop, and we will be here fighting until it does. This is a movement that was created for and by the people, and we have uplifted it with our own voices. Now is the time to get better organized. We've never seen the value of our vote as clearly as we did in 2020. Now, it's time for us to think strategically and enlist candidates that represent us. Candidates that are centered around the community and care about what the community wants. Candidates that we know will walk into the halls of power with our best interests in their hearts. If we encourage these masses of young people that we saw on the front lines, we'll have a new generation with a new perspective. They just need a little dose of wisdom to drop into that youthful energy, and we're going to have something amazing.

There's a video on YouTube of Nikki Giovanni in a conversation with James Baldwin that I love. They were friends, representing two generations, with very different views on the African American struggle. At one point Baldwin says, "You have no idea, and I can never express, how much I depend on you." He was talking about Giovanni's (younger) generation and the way they know themselves and their power with a clarity and vibrance his generation doesn't have. When I'm working with all the powerful young people around me, I feel the same way. This generation has a belief in fairness that simply won't be denied. I have faith that this is a moment when things will change because I see the fire of the young activists I work with, and I see that they will not be denied. The endurance and the quality of strategic thought I see in the movement space constantly dazzles me.

Activism is, literally, activating the people. As a result of the video, I get messages from people all over the world, and we have started to think together and to expand the brain trust for the work we all need to do. The power of technology to do work across vast distances is one of our best tools. All economically disadvantaged people share the same plight. The way racism might be enacted can vary from country to country, but the essence of it is always the same. Our ability to come together and build a common language for the problems we face is how we become bigger than our problems and bigger than our circumstances.

The scariest thing we can do in the United States is talk across ethnicity and class. When Martin Luther King Jr. *only* wanted equality, he was just a thorn in the side of American power, but when he started talking across race about the struggles of poor people, he was assassinated. Fred Hampton led the Black Panthers in Chicago, but it wasn't until he started the Rainbow Coalition, inviting poor whites and Latinx folks to join the conversation, that he too was assassinated. And yet intersectional, cross-cultural alliance is our best move forward.

One of the people I most admire is Rudy Lozano. Rudy was an activist in the 1970s and 1980s. A Latinx man, he formed a "Black-Brown Coalition," and they worked to take the seats of aldermen in Chicago. He recognized that no single minority group had the numbers or the power to significantly impact the city's politics, but if he could locate the common threads between the communities, they could be woven into a different version of power than the city had seen. His big win was getting Harold Washington elected as the first Black mayor of Chicago in 1983. He got to see Harold win, but he didn't get to see him take office because Rudy was murdered in his home, execution-style. Chicago is known for its deeply entrenched power elite, and clearly, some thought he was becoming too powerful. You may not have heard of Rudy Lozano, but here's what I will tell you: if you read Barack Obama's biography, he speaks about how he got into politics. He talks about arriving in Chicago and how excited he was seeing Harold Washington become the city's first Black mayor. Without Rudy Lozano, there is no Obama. When Obama was elected to Congress, he had the benefit of the coalition-building cultivated by Rudy.

Having been raised in Chicago, I've been able to see the power of enlarging community through coalition-building. It may be unique to Chicago that you die if you try it. I'm okay. I live in Atlanta now. But I do think this is our future. White supremacy is a busy little bastard, and one of its features is that it doesn't have preferences. It simply destroys whatever it focuses on. We need a unified front. We are stronger together. We are all, always, stronger together.

In *The Body Is Not an Apology*, Sonya Renee Taylor writes, "Unfortunately, white supremacist delusion has not only shaped how white people operate around race. It has shaped how people of color see, understand, and experience themselves and other communities of color."

To some, one of the more interesting details about me is that I speak Korean. My brother married a Korean woman, and when I lived with his family, my nieces were studying Korean, so I took lessons too. Speaking another language has been a door that has allowed me to know a little more and have better access to a rich culture. It's a privileged position because it helps me see the commonalities, but you don't have to learn another language to show up as a cross-cultural accomplice.

Black folks are only 14 percent of the US population, but we are not the only ones suffering at the hands of white supremacy. Throughout the COVID-19 pandemic, violence against Asian people steadily increased. It's been gratifying to see other Black folks standing with the Asian American and Pacific Islander (AAPI) communities and volunteering to help protect elders. It's a good step—just as it was when AAPI folks took to the streets and spoke out against police violence—and there's plenty more to do. When we understand that our future is together, we begin making choices that help us see each other better. We need that. We all have to do better with each other in order to build alliances for the future. I would love to see intercultural conversations across communities now so when we're thrown into crisis, as we were in the aftermath of George Floyd's murder, we already trust each other, and we already have the shared vision of how we will work together. This is the time to begin working in solidarity on issues that cross communities, such as food security or homelessness prevention.

We are at a turning point. If you are not part of a community of color, this may look (from the outside) like other moments in which some people pushed to have the same rights as other people, and those other people pushed back. It may look like angry people trying to get their voices heard, and maybe, if a few token gestures are made, they'll be pacified enough that things can return to normal. That's happened before. This is not that.

When I recorded the video and it went viral, I was speaking the truth of the history of Black people on American soil, with all the anger we feel about how we've been treated. Later, I wished I had said, "They are lucky that what Black people are looking for is EQUITY and not revenge," instead of saying "equality." The Civil Rights Movement of the 1960s was about equality. This fight, this moment, is about equity. Some 60 years ago, we were fighting simply to have the same rights and protections the Constitution guarantees every citizen. And after 350 years in America, it appeared as though we would finally have an even field to play on. What immediately became obvious is that the field can't be made even if advantage is baked so deep into every system that for a person in Black skin, it simply is not possible to live, from the cradle to the grave, in the same ways and on the same terms as a white person can live. That is not fair. It is not equitable.

America has proven itself more than capable of dishonoring its own stated values, but we won't let it. In that sense, Black people are the living conscience of this country. When you hear that a group is only as strong as its weakest member, recognize that a group is only as healthy as its treatment of its weakest. The Black community is not weak because it isn't made of strong stuff. It's weak because it has constantly been hobbled in every possible way. And now it's time for that to stop.

Most white allies have blank receipts. I can appreciate the spirit and intention of white allies who share my messages and say they stand with our efforts to achieve equity, but what is lip service actually worth? It is a truth that the disease of racism must be treated by white people talking to other white people. White racism is none of my business. Likewise, you don't get points for having the conversations with your friends and family that you must have if you're going to live in integrity with the truth. That's your job. For yourself. You are not doing Black people a favor by addressing your own racism. You are simply saving your own soul.

Allyship makes me think of linking up with your favorite cousins at Grandma's house. When a fight erupts over toys, at least three kids run to rat to Grandma, who then shares lessons on diplomacy. Everyone is prepared to push through the evening because, above all, everyone wants to see the cousins have a good time and enjoy themselves. It's about facing what happens without failing to learn.

This doesn't mean inequities don't exist among the cousins. One may live with Grandma because of a nonfunctioning parent, a pain point, but in this house, they have the privilege because it's their room and their toys. They can dictate the rules—rules negotiated with Grandma for their benefit. We all have things that set us back; we all have some measure of power.

The greatest allies make me think of the best cousins—the ones who share, offer snacks and go grab the shy cousin who is sitting alone and convince them to play. Allies correct the misbehaving cousin while at the same time offering them a road to redemption.

This is work everyone can do, and everyone should. It's because of the best cousin's care that twenty years later, the whole family is still sitting together at reunions and weddings—

not because they all have the perfect relationships, but because they know how to work together. Their intent is continually showcased in their actions.

But what are white allies doing about the fact that Black people are still dying at police hands and qualified immunity is protecting those police? Breonna Taylor was killed in her sleep by police, and those police are going to work each day and home with their families every night. A majority of US states are trying to disenfranchise voters of color after the 2020 election. Where is white outrage? If the disenfranchisement succeeds, it will be a betrayal of the core values of the Constitution. Who gets to say they love this country if they are willing to watch it sell itself out? And for what? To keep the people who built this country from having a say about its future? Look in the mirror. Who are you? What are you willing to stand for? I would love to see you on the front lines, standing with us for equity and the value of our lives. I'm also a practical woman. I urge white allies to put their money where their mouths are. There is a lot of work to be done and plenty of good organizations working. If you say you don't have time to join them, contribute. Now that you understand how you benefit from systems that guaranteed your access to resources, give some back.

Among ourselves and for ourselves, we have a lot of work to do. We have to build trust when so many American systems have been built to divide and conquer us. White people make distinctions of class because there are distinct differences. However, we also know that it doesn't matter how elite the school you went to was, no taxi driver will stop for you, and you can be killed anytime, anywhere, because of the color of your skin. Let's understand that if you were at the expensive school, we need your voice and your access. If your underfunded public school had terrible teachers and you barely graduated, we need your creativity and survival skills because you wouldn't have made it this far without having plenty. Our road is together, and we have to find better ways to see and include each other. We have to meet our sisters and brothers where they are, and welcome whatever they have to offer.

As I think about our activist future, I worry about cancel culture. It's becoming a cancer in our movements. The people who lead in the movement space are not messiahs. We are all just humans trying to do the work that's important to us. It's an offering to our communities. We hope we get it right; we may get it wrong. That's how it goes with humans. We are all flawed, and if you dig deep enough or come with enough judgment, it will always be easy to find a reason to drag any one of us. But why? My worry is that we are creating a climate in which people won't come forward to offer their best on behalf of us all because they're worried about being exposed—as being flawed in any of the multitude of ways humans are. We can't elevate people's flaws above their work. We can't.

Between us, it's time to speak the truth. Not to win or be right, but in the hope that the truth will be the foundation for resolution. We have to learn to set our egos aside. Respect is such a big deal in our communities, and this can be hard to do, but we have to dare to be soft and open with each other. Decide to stand up for what is best and right, even if it isn't your idea. We have to start showing the next generation that conceding to the best idea is not a sign of weakness. It is actually one of the greatest demonstrations of strength because it means that your spirit is so determined to stand for healing and change that even when a great idea isn't yours, you can support it and serve it. This is what it looks like when we're no longer using ego as protection against all the ways we feel vulnerable. Be willing to change and grow, into who you have to be to learn what you need to, in order to show up as the best version of yourself. We need that person. Be that one.

Watching the protests of 2020 and seeing that they were multiracial and multicultural, cutting across age and class, I believe that most people understand the atrocities Black people have withstood in this country. And more importantly, they see that the deepest changes made by the government have been so eroded that we are nearly back to where we have been since Reconstruction, with cosmetic differences. But people are lazy and shockingly willing to keep a corrupt system that serves those in power simply to protect the status quo. Most people live in a bubble, and they choose to block out the noise until it's on their doorstep. Until they can't avoid hearing it. If you watch the news, if you read the news, you know the world you're living in. What will you do about it? The truth of the African American experience is that we. Are. Here. We have always been here. We have, effectively, always been in the stolen, settled America. And we're not going anywhere.

When I speak about the journey that Black people are on, I have to remind people that there is nothing in this country that we haven't had a hand in. The labor that built the wealth of this nation? That's us. The culture of this country? Look anywhere; name anything. We are part of that story. Elevating it, refining it, making it better. Making it sexy. Making it important. That's us. We have our stake in America—our stake in being here and being recognized here, in living in peace in this country. We have already paid the price of admission. We have already built the house everyone lives in. We have every right to hold the people who govern us accountable for making a space for us at the table. And we know, as we've proven time and time again, if we can get a seat, we can run some shit.

I don't believe that people have a problem recognizing our claim. I believe that a great number of white people are afraid of what it will look like when we live in an equitable state of existence. And they are afraid that we will be to them as they were to us. History doesn't bear that out. As I said in the video, they are lucky we want equality/equity and not revenge. Part of what I feel in this struggle for equity is a complete refusal to be held captive by white fear. White fear of me. White fear of history. White fear of the skeletons and ghosts in white closets. Those are not our business. And we do not have to attend to them.

There's a comic strip turned meme I like in which one neighbor wants to know what the other one is doing. The second neighbor says, "This house is on fire, so we're going to help them put it out." And the first says, "What about my house, doesn't it matter?" When her neighbor points out that her house is NOT on fire, the first neighbor responds with "All houses matter." I love this because it perfectly illustrates our situation. When someone says, "All lives matter," it's not that they don't . . . but it's beside the point. Black lives are the ones under siege. Black lives are the house on fire.

After four hundred years of systemic racism, oppression and brutalization, the house is almost burned to the ground. The fight for equity is the fight to rebuild. I have to rebuild my house. I have to look out for my brother. I have to be concerned about my sister. And those that can't understand that, and don't want to come over here and pick up some tools and do some work, should move on.

Despite all of this, I feel hopeful that we're headed to a happier, healthier America. What the civil unrest of 2020 proved to me is that we're not in this alone. As a result of my video, I have had the privilege of speaking with people all over the world who feel the resonance of our fight with the issues they face. Excessive policing, racial profiling, being forced to live like your life doesn't matter, America didn't invent that. Colonialism did. But nowhere has it been doubled down on and amplified the way it has been here. After George Floyd's and Breonna Taylor's deaths, I traveled with The People's Uprising to protest and support resistance all over the country. The energy, the focus, the level of discourse about where we are and where we are trying to go lifted my heart.

Those who believe in justice and equity recognize that the cognitive dissonance of the racial wealth gap and the disparities between the treatment of people of color and white people can no longer be tolerated. I'm grateful to have seen the world cry out on our behalf in my lifetime. But that's not where this ends. This is the beginning. That cry has been so loud that I do not believe it can be silenced, and I do not believe the movement and the momentum it suggests can be stopped. I am here for that journey.

My real ambition is to finish my life as a sage, old, proud Black lady in a flowered housecoat and leather slippers, cooling myself with an MLK church fan while sharing centuries of old wisdom via stories, sayings, expressions and catchphrases. And doing all of this while sitting on my porch swing with some sweet tea in a mason jar. It sounds like a stereotype, but just because it IS a stereotype doesn't mean it doesn't have great, world-changing value.

Time has proven that the arc of history bends in the direction of greater access, openness and justice. I have no doubt that the inevitable future for people of color is greater equity in our American lives. This is the work before us. And the sooner we can get it done, the sooner I can go sit on my porch. Let's get to work.

IN MEMORIAM

BLACK COMMUNITIES THAT WERE VICTIMS OF MASSACRES AND OTHER ATROCITIES

As noted earlier, the massacres at Tulsa, Oklahoma, and Rose-wood, Florida, are far from isolated events in which thriving Black communities were destroyed by white mobs. In addition to the loss of life, these areas suffered irrecoverable financial losses that reverberated for generations and continue to do so today. Even harder to calculate is the property and neighborhoods lost to legal tactics such as redlining and imminent domain. Sometimes the assailants didn't even need weapons to commit economic mass murder. On her show, comedian Amber Ruffin exposed a hidden history of forcibly removing Black people from areas by flooding them with so much water that they became "drowned towns," forgotten under manmade lakes. What follows is a list of many, but surely not all of the communities we've lost.

MASSACRES AND BANISHMENTS

Seneca Village (Central Park), 1857

New York, NY, 1863

Memphis, TN, 1866

New Orleans, LA, 1866

Camilla, GA, 1868

Opelousas, LA, 1868

St. Bernard Parish, LA, 1868

Colfax, LA, 1873

Eufaula, AL, 1874

Vicksburg, MS, 1874

Clinton, MS, 1875

Thibodaux, LA, 1887

Wilmington, NC, 1898

Pierce City, MO, 1901

Harrison, AR, 1905, 1909

Atlanta, GA, 1906

Springfield, IL, 1908

Slocum, TX, 1910

Forsyth County, GA, 1912

Ludlow, CO, 1914

East St. Louis, IL, 1917

Chicago, IL, 1919

Elaine, AR, 1919

Washington, D.C., 1919

Ocoee, FL, 1920

Tulsa, OK, 1921

Rosewood, FL, 1923

Catcher, AR, 1923

Detroit, MI, 1943

Philadelphia, PA, 1985

Charleston, SC, 2015

DROWNED TOWNS

York Hill, NY (Central Park Reservoir), 1842

Brown's Station, NY (Ashokan Reservoir), 1912

Warren, MD (Loch Raven Reservoir), 1922

Kowaliga, AL (Lake Martin), 1926

Jerusalem, CT (Candlewood Lake), 1928

Henry and McKee Islands, AL (Guntersville Dam), 1939

Kennett, CA (Lake Shasta), 1940

Morley, CA (Lake Shasta), 1940

Vanport, OR (Delta Park), 1948

Old Neversink, NY (Neversink Reservoir), 1953

Oscarville, GA (Now Lake Lanier), 1959

Dillon, CO (Dillon Reservoir), 1960

Round Valley, NJ (Round Valley Reservoir), 1960

Prentiss, MS (Napoleon Channel), 1963

Old Fairfield, IN (Brookville Lake), 1965

Sapinero, CO (Blue Mesa Reservoir), 1966

FURTHER READING

Alexander, Cedric. *The New Guardians: Policing in America's Communities for the 21st Century.* Self-published, Create-Space, 2016.

Alexander, Michelle. *The New Jim Crow: Mass Incarceration in the Age of Colorblindness.* New York: New Press, 2010.

August, Byron G., Bryan Hancock, and Martha Laboissiere. "The Economic Cost of the US Education Gap." McKinsey & Company, June 1, 2009.

Baldwin, James. *The Evidence of Things Not Seen.* New York: Holt, Rinehart and Winston, 1985.

———. *The Fire Next Time.* New York: Dial, 1963.

Baldwin, James, and Nikki Giovanni. *A Dialogue: James Baldwin and Nikki Giovanni.* Philadelphia and New York: J. B. Lippincott, 1973.

Baradaran, Mehrsa. *How the Other Half Banks: Exclusion, Exploitation, and the Threat to Democracy.* Cambridge, MA: Harvard University Press, 2015.

———. *The Color of Money: Black Banks and the Racial Wealth Gap.* Cambridge, MA: Harvard University Press, 2017.

brown, adrienne maree. *Emergent Strategy: Shaping Change, Changing Worlds.* Chico, CA: AK Press, 2017.

Brown, Claude. *Manchild in the Promised Land.* New York: Macmillan, 1965.

Coates, Ta-Nehisi. *Between the World and Me.* New York: Spiegel & Grau, 2015.

Davis, Angela Y. *Are Prisons Obsolete?* New York: Seven Stories Press, 2003.

———. *Abolition Democracy: Beyond Empire, Prisons, and Torture.* New York: Seven Stories Press, 2005.

Du Bois, W. E. B. *Black Reconstruction: An Essay Toward a History of the Part Which Black Folk Played in the Attempt to Reconstruct Democracy in America, 1860–1880.* New York: Harcourt Brace & Company, 1935.

Haley, Alex and Malcolm X. *The Autobiography of Malcolm X: As Told to Alex Haley.* New York: Ballantine, 1965.

Kaba, Mariame. *We Do This 'Til We Free Us: Abolitionist Organizing and Transforming Justice.* Chicago: Haymarket, 2021.

Kendi, Ibram X. *Stamped from the Beginning: The Definitive History of Racist Ideas in America.* New York: Nation Books, 2016.

————. *How to Be an Antiracist*. New York: One World, 2019.

McClain, Dani. *We Live for the We: The Political Power of Black Motherhood*. New York: Bold Type, 2019.

McGhee, Heather. *The Sum of Us: What Racism Costs Everyone and How We Can Prosper Together*. New York: One World, 2021.

McIntosh, Kriston, Emily Moss, Ryan Nunn, and Jay Shambaugh. "Examining the Black-White Wealth Gap." Brookings Institution, February 27, 2020.

Meckler, Laura. "Report Finds $23 Billion Racial Funding Gap for Schools." Washington Post, February 26, 2019.

Menakem, Resmaa. *My Grandmother's Hands: Racialized Trauma and the Pathway to Mending Our Hearts and Bodies*. Las Vegas, NV: Central Recovery Press, 2017.

Muhammad, Khalil Gibran. *The Condemnation of Blackness: Race, Crime, and the Making of Modern Urban America*. Cambridge, MA: Harvard University Press, 2010.

Noah, Trevor. *Born a Crime: Stories from a South African Childhood*. New York: One World, 2016.

Oklahoma Commission to Study the Tulsa Race Riot of 1921. *Tulsa Race Riot*. February 28, 2001.

Ray, Rashawn and Andre M. Perry. "Why We Need Reparations for Black Americans." Brookings Institution. April 15, 2020.

Saad, Layla F. *Me and White Supremacy: Combat Racism,*

Change the World, and Become a Good Ancestor. Naperville, IL: Sourcebooks, 2020.

Shakur, Assata. *Assata: An Autobiography*. London: Zed Books, 1987.

Stevenson, Bryan. *Just Mercy: A Story of Justice and Redemption*. New York: Spiegel & Grau, 2014.

Stewart, Shelley, III, Michael Chui, James Manyika, JP Julien, Vivian Hunt, Bob Sternfels, Jonathan Woetzel, and Hai-yang Zhang. "The Economic State of Black America: What Is and What Could Be." McKinsey & Company, June 17, 2021.

Taylor, Sonya Renee. *The Body Is Not an Apology: The Power of Radical Self-Love*. Oakland, CA: Berrett-Koehler, 2018.

ACKNOWLEDGMENTS

This book feels like a lifelong work, so forgive me if I forget anyone. Charge it to my head and not my heart. These are ideas that were cultivated via my lived interactions with teachers, friends, mentors, comrades, rappers, talk show hosts, homeless citizens, family members, editors, researchers, students, internet trolls, former lovers, both sides of the political aisle, strippers, actors, cashiers, Uber drivers, pets and a host more. Even if I don't name you, you affected me, and I thank you.

Special thanks in particular to my Henry Holt family, who believed in this book and showcased the patience of Job as I continued to protest, make content, lecture, rally and tend to a sick parent, all while trying to finish these pages. So, props to Amy Einhorn, Sarah Crichton, Natalia Ruiz, Maggie Richards, Jason Liebman, Hannah Campbell, Kenn Russell, Omar Chapa, Eva Maria Diaz, Christopher Sergio, Karen Horton, Caitlin O'Shaughnessy, Patricia Eisemann, Carolyn O'Keefe, Devon Mazzone, Pauline Post, Flora Esterly, Anaka Allen and Jeanwon Kim.

A very special thanks to Nzingha Clarke for helping me to bring all the philosophies in my head to written fruition. Retha Powers, I couldn't love you more if I tried. You are absolutely a Godsend of an editor, and I just want to make stories with you for the rest of my life. I could not be more grateful for my agent, LaToya Smith, who makes me feel like I could conquer the world.

Rest in peace to my mother, Lula Jones-Holt, who provided me with every resource she could find, making me the woman I am today. To my siblings, Darie and Audra, I appreciate how much you have my back. To my son, Drake, who shares me with the world without complaint, you are the greatest gift I've ever received.

I'm just going to list the people I super love who were significant during the writing of this book because, thankfully, my squad is huge: Pastor David, Taylor "T Dawg Da Don" Butler, Ikeeah White, Reasha Donaldson, Corey Sapp, Alvin Agarrat, Tara Bell, Reshina Bryant, Richard Bryant, Leigh Peeler, Gilly Segal, Ebony Jones, Gayatri Sethi, Alex Mitchell, Tanji Harper, Kevin Bryant, Edward Trader, Ernesto Yerena Montejano and e.E. Charlton-Trujillo. Also, I could not survive this life without the members of the two organizations I belong to: Revolutionary Healing and The People's Uprising.

To George Floyd, Breonna Taylor, Ahmaud Arbery and Rayshard Brooks, I mourn the immeasurable loss suffered by your families, and I honor you for being the catalysts that sparked an international movement that changed the world forever.

Last, but most certainly not least, my gurus—teachers who expanded and cultivated my point of view, in person or through their work: Willie Beatrice Barrow, Gary Chambers, Monteria Robinson, Yonasda Lonewolf, Carolyn Lumpkin, 19Keys, Rudy Lozano, Henry Louis Gates Jr., W. E. B. Du Bois and James Baldwin.

ABOUT THE AUTHOR

Kimberly Jones is an activist, a writer, a former book-seller and the host of the Well-Read Black Girl book club's Atlanta chapter. She has directed feature films and a cutting-edge diverse web series and is also co-author of the bestselling young adult novels *I'm Not Dying with You Tonight* (an NAACP Image Award finalist) and *Why We Fly*.